MARRIAGE
101

BIBLE GUIDES FOR LIFE

MARRIAGE 101

BARBOUR
PUBLISHING

CONTENTS

. . .sitting in a tree,
K-I-S-S-I-N-G.
First comes love,
then comes marriage,
then comes junior in the baby carriage. . .

You've come a long way since grade school. You've matured, made some choices, and carved out a life of your own. As part of that life, you've entered (or are about to enter) one of the greatest challenges of your life. Marriage.

Filled with laughs and triumphs, marriage is a special partnership that God gives two people. But marriage isn't always upbeat and easy. Sometimes the joys and emotional heights give way to tears, anger, and misunderstanding.

Over the years, your marriage will change as life grows more complicated. But that's not bad because over the years your marriage can become deeper, too. Through those times you'll need encouragement and help as you uncover new challenges and discover new questions.

Whether you need rules about "fighting fair" or dealing with children, or you simply need encouragement to make your marriage better, this book can help. Inside, you'll find:

Catch a Clue

You'll learn tips from people who have been married for years and *they still enjoy it*. You'll find clues to help your own marriage.

Wide Angle

We easily get caught up in the details of day-to-day living. To have the best marriage, though, we sometimes need help looking at the whole picture. We'll help you take a step back.

Wow!

The topic of marriage leads to some fascinating stories and great quotes. We've collected a few choice pieces for you to enjoy.

Don't Forget

Certain tips are important to remember through the years. We've highlighted those for you.

The Bottom Line

We'll help you get beyond confusion by letting you know the most important stuff to remember.

What the Bible Says

We've highlighted a few key verses that will help you understand what the Bible has to say about your marriage.

Marriage is a big subject, and you probably have lots of questions. The good news is that many of them are about to be answered. There's just one thing you need to do: read this book. Feel free to read it your way: from cover to cover or skipping around to the parts that interest you most. No matter how you read it, you'll find it's jammed with good advice, great ideas, and entertaining thoughts. So turn the page and start reading. . . . You'll be glad you did!

1

WELCOME
TO MARRIAGE

Now That the Knot Has Been Tied

Being a newlywed is simple and fun. The emotions and passions run high. Sometimes *bliss* is the best description. But over time the emotions wane. Trouble awaits those who think that when their emotions falter, their love falters, too. Love goes well beyond the gooey feeling you felt when you first locked eyes.

True love, while it enjoys feelings, is based on commitment to each other. That's why you took wedding *vows*. C. S. Lewis wrote in *Mere Christianity*:

> *People get from books the idea that if you have married the right person you may expect to go on "being in love" for ever. As a result, when they find that they are not, they think this proves they have made a mistake and are entitled to a change—not realizing that, when they have changed, the glamour will presently go out of the new love just as it went out of the old one.*

This transformation—from deep emotion to deep commitment—is often difficult for newlyweds to understand, appreciate, or look forward to. But it's a good change that leads to *deeper* love and a *richer* marriage.

Sailing along the way is not always smooth. To develop a deeper commitment, you need to choose to be more committed. That means that you choose to love when life gets hard and you don't *feel* like loving.

MILE MARKERS

Some marriage counselors point to different marital mile markers. These are passages that many married couples sail through—some more smoothly than others. Each passage allows for a deeper commitment and a richer love. While you can't tie any of these passages to a calendar, generally speaking, they happen like this:

THREE MONTHS

Couples struggle with maintaining the friendships they had when they got married. A new husband and wife are still adjusting to a new home and a new set of in-laws. They're deciding what to spend money on and what color the new couch should be. Couples are still adjusting their sexual expectations and getting used to having each other around all the time. Couples are learning

FEELING IN LOVE

"What we call 'being in love' is a glorious state, and, in several ways, good for us. . . . Being in love is a good thing, but it is not the best thing, there are many things below it, but there are also things above it. You cannot make it the basis of a whole life. It is a noble feeling, but it is still a feeling. Now no feeling can be relied on to last in its full intensity, or even to last at all. Knowledge can last, principles can last, habits can last; but feelings come and go. And in fact, whatever people say, the state called 'being in love' usually does not last. If the old fairy tale ending 'they lived happily ever after' is taken to mean, 'They felt for the next fifty years exactly as they felt the day before they were married,' then it says what probably never was nor ever could be true, and would be highly undesirable if it were. Who could bear to live in that excitement for even five years? What would become of your work, your appetite, your sleep, your friendships? But, of course, ceasing to be 'in love' need not mean ceasing to love. Love in this second sense—love as distinct from 'being in love'—is not merely a feeling. It is a deep unity, maintained by the will and deliberately strengthened by habit; reinforced by (in Christian marriages) the grace which both partners ask, and receive, from God. They can have this love for each other even at those moments when they do not like each other; as you love yourself even when you do not like yourself. . . . 'Being in Love' first moved them to promise fidelity: this quiet love enables them to keep the promise. It is on this love that the engine of marriage is run: being in love was the explosion that started it."

—C. S. Lewis, *Mere Christianity*

how to resolve conflict together and need to continue to develop their communication skills.

ABOUT TWO YEARS

The first child is born, on the way, or has been planned for. Sometimes this corresponds with a move to a bigger apartment or house. Complicating this life change is often a promotion or career change.

THE SEVEN-YEAR ITCH

About seven years into marriage, some couples grow bored. Life becomes routine and that newlywed feeling begins to wane. Counselor Arlene Kagle was quoted in *People* magazine as saying:

 THE ITCH

"More often than not, it happens. In the course of marriage, a seven-year hitch is marked by the onset of the seven-year itch, a malady unknown to dermatologists but familiar to marriage counselors and victims of the disease. Symptoms: He stops holding the door and starts pointing to it; she stops making dinner and starts making reservations; he stops calling her dear and starts calling her expensive. This can apply to anyone."

—Joanne Kaufman, Laura Sanderson Healy, and Rosemary Thorpe-Tracey, quoted in *People* magazine

The seven-year itch begins long before the seventh year. . . . At some point after a couple has been married for two or three years, and the sense of joy, relief and excitement at finding someone to share your life with has waned, each person comes up against some part of the other person that they don't like and can't change. Some couples resolve all this. They change, they compromise. Sometimes the issue is postponed. When the issues are well resolved, it brings couples to an even deeper level of closeness and commitment. If they're not resolved well, they can be the seeds for divorce.

ABOUT FIFTEEN YEARS

Life together grows more and more routine. The kids are in grade school or junior high. Small, irritating habits that were once overlooked now take on a new magnitude. Comedian Bill Cosby, in *Love and Marriage*, uses one example as he sums up how marriages change after fifteen years:

> *Marriage [is] strained through the years. . .[when] there is a change in that both of you have in your view of snoring. In the early years, snoring by one of you moves the listener to gently touch the other and say, "Honey, you're snoring. Not that I mind it of course—in fact, it's a Mozart serenade—but medical studies have revealed that there's a certain harm to the snorer. Something about the vibration dislodging the brain."*
>
> *And the snorer smilingly replies, "Did I ever tell you how much I love you when you wake me from a deep sleep? I really hate sleeping too long at one time because it keeps me away from you."*
>
> *After fifteen years, however, the snorer is not only touched: he is rolled onto the floor.*

Love goes beyond bliss to commitment. Most likely you will enjoy the emotions of love from time to time, but the foundation will be your commitment and your promise to love.

THE EMPTY NEST

The kids are grown and gone. College bills put a strain on finances, as does planning for retirement. Counselors who work on college campuses often counsel students whose parents don't steer this new passage well.

Not one of these passages is invariably fatal. Each is an opportunity for deeper love. Perhaps you're just entering marriage now and don't know what the future holds. Or perhaps you're a veteran and have weathered some of the passages above. Either way, the challenge before you is the same—to love more deeply today than you did yesterday.

2

BUILDING A
MARRIAGE THAT STANDS

What the Bible Says about Marriage

Long before there were such things as nations or churches, even before wedding consultants and bridal showers and the publication of the first *Modern Bride* magazine, God established the institution of marriage.

In fact, it's in the first two chapters of the very first book of the Bible that we find the breathtaking account of God creating a man and woman, bringing them together, and, in essence, performing the first wedding ceremony. (Imagine how much they saved on flowers and invitations alone!)

Clearly, marriage is the most fundamental of all human relations. And the first few pages of scripture give us some important clues about how things were meant to be.

After the first man had spent an entire day naming the animals (see Genesis 2:19), he felt lonely, realizing he was the only creature in Eden without a mate similar to himself. Adam's deep sense of incompleteness did not escape God's notice: "The LORD God said, 'It is not good for the man to be alone. I will make a helper suitable for him'" (v. 18).

It's worth noting that this is the first time in the biblical record that the Lord declared something about His creation "not good." In His goodness, God quickly moved to remedy the situation.

As one comedian has put it, "God administered the first anesthetic," putting Adam into a deep sleep. Then the Creator took a part of the man—not from his head to rule over him, nor from his feet to be trampled upon, but from his side, close to his heart. And with this part (most translations refer to it as a "rib") God "made a woman. . .and. . .brought her to the man."

In exultation the man immediately recognized that this lovely creature was unlike anything else on all the earth. At this point in the written record, the Hebrew becomes difficult to translate, prompting some scholars to speculate that perhaps the best rendering for Adam's response to seeing Eve for the first time was, literally, "Wow!"

The author of this narrative (probably Moses) then inserts his own editorial comment, a passage that was quoted by Jesus Christ and has been cited in millions of wedding ceremonies down through the ages: "For this reason a man will leave his father and mother and be united to his wife, and they will become one flesh" (Genesis 2:24).

The chapter closes with the observation that "the man and his wife were both naked, and they felt no shame" (2:25).

Chapter 1, a more concise overview of creation, concludes with God looking over all that He has made (including His male and female human creatures) and saying that "it was *very* good" (emphasis added). Contrast this with His daily evaluation of "it was good" after each of the other days of creation.

Here, in just a couple of chapters, is a whole course in God's plan for marriage. Genesis 1–2 serve as a primer in what marriage is meant to be. If we want to build marriages that stand (and who doesn't?), we need to review the great marital truths found in the opening pages of the Bible.

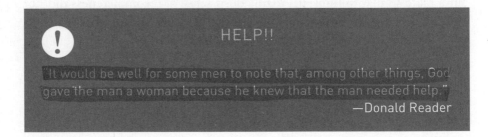

HELP!!

"It would be well for some men to note that, among other things, God gave the man a woman because he knew that the man needed help."
—Donald Reader

1. Marriage is God's idea.

According to the Bible, marriage is not a human invention. It was instituted by God Himself. Therefore, we cannot and should not dismiss it, diminish it, or degrade it in any way.

It follows also that, as the Designer, God knows best about how marriage can and should work. Maybe fewer marriages would falter and fail if more participants would consult the Creator of marriage.

WHY DO PEOPLE GET MARRIED?

Rank the following reasons 1–10, with 1 representing what you think most people would honestly state as their top reason for getting married, and 10 being the least likely reason people "engage in holy matrimony."

_____ To produce offspring
_____ Societal expectations/ family pressure
_____ Love (or infatuation)
_____ Companionship
_____ Sex (regular, guilt-free)
_____ A feeling of incompleteness

_____ To find someone to take care of them
_____ For financial reasons
_____ To glorify God
_____ To satisfy a nagging boyfriend/girlfriend

2. All that God created is good, but marriage is seen by God as "very good."

Contrast this with the way our culture makes light of marriage. "Holy matrimony" is viewed with disdain. It is scoffed at and treated lightly. It is the butt of jokes on sitcoms, fodder for stand-up comics. We need to remember that marriage is from a perfectly wise God—not something that we can "improve" upon.

3. God created Eve and brought her into Adam's life because, frankly, Adam was incomplete and in need of help.

God has created people (and men are not an exception to this rule) to need human companionship. We are not self-sufficient. We need "helpers" in our lives. Marriage is the quintessential example of the truth that "no man is an island."

Note: The word "helper" used to describe the first woman is in no way derogatory. In fact, this same Hebrew term is applied to God in the Old Testament (see Psalms 33:20; 70:5)!

4. Marriage, at its core, is about companionship.

Emotionally, spiritually, and (obviously!) physically God made the woman to be "suitable" for the man. Literally, the idea is that He created a female mate who would "correspond" to the male. The idea is that, sharing the same nature, they are able to complement one another, fitting together, filling up the empty spaces in each other's lives.

In a good marriage, the two individuals join lives and are more effective and fruitful together than they ever could have been alone.

5. Marriage, by design, is intended for one husband and one wife, for life.

Did you catch the wording? "For this reason a man [a singular male] will leave his father and mother and be united to his wife [a singular female]" (Genesis 2:24). In Matthew 19, Jesus quoted this verse and added that such a divine union should not be dissolved by men.

No other arrangement can possibly honor God.

6. Marriage involves the establishment of a brand-new household.

God's intent is for newlyweds to leave their former individual lives behind and to begin a new kind of existence together ("leaving and cleaving"). The new family is to take precedence over their families of origin. Many marital problems could be eliminated if couples understood this truth.

7. Marriage is intended to be an intimate union.

The idea that the two "will become one flesh" implies more than physical relations. It suggests a deep unity and intimacy, a commingling of lives. The reference to Adam and Eve being naked and unashamed is a wordplay meant to contrast with the craftiness of the serpent who appears in the first verse of the next chapter. This demonstrates the kind of others-centeredness and innocent trust that was possible before sin entered the world. It should be noted that couples can, in Christ, enjoy a wonderful measure of this kind of emotional transparency and spiritual intimacy.

MARRIAGE IS MEANT TO BE A LIFELONG ARRANGEMENT

God says, "I hate divorce."
Malachi 2:16

Jesus says, "What God has joined together,
let man not separate."
Matthew 19:6

Foundations for a Good Home

To hear our politicians tell it, financial security is the greatest need of the modern family. High wages, low unemployment, low inflation, low interest rates, affordable health care, accessible child care (so both parents can work), more tax cuts—ad nauseam.

To be sure, financial problems *can* put a severe strain on a marriage, but then, so can prosperity. Think of all the couples you know who would be considered economically successful. Now consider how many of those same couples are in domestic disaster.

The point? There's more, *much more*, to a good marriage/home than money. Instead of buying into our materialistic culture's obsession with economic prosperity and financial success, why not try on the following "family values"?

Actually, these are less "values" than they are *commitments*. Here are the seven foundational commitments that have been proven through the ages to bring about marital fulfillment (and that can be remembered by the acrostic S-U-C-C-E-S-S):

1. The Commitment to Selflessness

We live in a selfish age. And frankly, it is the attitude of selfishness that is behind most every marital conflict. God's Word offers us a different and a better way: "Do nothing from selfishness; but with humility of mind, let each of you regard one another as more important than himself" (Philippians 2:3 NASB).

Selfishness may be natural, but unselfishness is supernatural—meaning Christians have the resources to put others first. This is the first ingredient to success in marriage.

2. The Commitment to Unconditional Love

Our world speaks of a love based on feelings, a love that comes and goes. God, however, calls husbands and wives to love each other with no strings attached—even when you don't feel like it, or when your spouse isn't being very lovable.

Think about the marriage vows you took (you probably WEREN'T thinking real clearly when you first made them!): "for better, for worse, for richer, for poorer, in sickness and in health, to love and to cherish, till death do us part."

Whoa! Most individuals (in their flowing dresses and handsome tuxes) aren't really considering the negative side of those promises when they're standing amid the ferns and lilies. But like it or not, these vows are without exception.

Only this kind of committed love can see a marriage successfully through the rough times of life.

LET GOD BE THE ARCHITECT AND BUILDER OF YOUR MARRIAGE!

"Unless the LORD builds the house, its builders labor in vain. Unless the LORD watches over the city, the watchmen stand guard in vain."

Psalm 127:1

"I am the vine; you are the branches. If a man remains in me and I in him, he will bear much fruit; apart from me you can do nothing."

John 15:5

3. The Commitment to Communication

Surprise! There's not a married person on earth who has the ability to read his or her spouse's mind. Therefore, if you want a successful marriage—and of course you do—it is imperative that you talk to each other—about everything.

Your communication must be both truthful and tender—especially as you develop the delicate skill of resolving conflicts (see chapter 9, "Communication Tips").

If you keep the lines of communication open, God's Word suggests you will be well on the way to a successful and happy marriage.

4. The Commitment to Christ

This commitment stands fourth, in the center of our acronym SUCCESS, because Jesus Christ must be at the very center of a life and of a marriage before that relationship can be truly happy and successful.

As husbands and wives come to know Jesus more deeply, they discover that He not only leads them, but also meets the deepest needs of their hearts. When their limited resources of love and patience and wisdom are depleted, they find that He is able and willing to give them whatever they need. It's Christ and Christ alone who can make a marriage go the distance, and make it a wonderful journey!

5. The Commitment to Each Other

It's no secret that our culture is not kind to marriage. Forces are constantly at work, seeking to pull husbands and wives apart.

And so it is imperative that couples guard their relationship—especially in the first years when they are laying the foundation of their marriage and establishing habits that, in many cases, will last for a lifetime. Don't allow a career or outside distractions or other relationships or busy schedules to jumble your priorities. After your commitment to Christ, your highest commitment should be to each other.

Circle the words that best describe how you feel about (or in) your marriage right now:

TIRED	CONFUSED	IRRITATED
ANGRY	SCARED	BITTER
CONCERNED	SAD	EXCITED
PESSIMISTIC	IN-THE-DUMPS	BLAH
ENCOURAGED	DEFEATED	LONLEY
ANXIOUS	DISCOURAGED	SENTIMENTAL
OPTIMISTIC	UPBEAT	PASSIONATE
INDIFFERENT	ZEALOUS	CALLOUS
LISTLESS	UNFEELING	EXUBERANT
GUILTY	DISTURBED	THRILLED
DEPRESSED	OVERWHELMED	WORRIED
CALM	HAPPY	ANNOYED
JUBILANT	GLAD	DESPAIRING
BORED	TORMENTED	DISGUSTED
CONTENTED	DISCONTENTED	CRANKY
GRIM	EXHILARATED	DISSATISFIED
TEARFUL	PLAYFUL	ENTHUSED
MOTIVATED	RELIEVED	HOPEFUL
CONFIDENT	AMAZED	GRATEFUL
REJECTED	MISUNDERSTOOD	MISTREATED
NUMB	DISAPPOINTED	RESENTFUL

6. The Commitment to Servanthood

Jesus said he came "not to *be* served, but to serve." He also said that "It is more blessed to give than to receive."

The happiest, most successful couples in this world constantly look for ways they can serve each other. Remember the cartoon chipmunks Chip and Dale? Remember how incredibly polite they were to each other? Every time they came to a doorway: "After you!" "Oh no! After *you!*" This should be your mutual goal from your wedding day forward—to outdo each other in service.

7. The Commitment to Sharing with Others

As individuals who know Jesus Christ and who love Him and desire to serve Him with your lives, make it your goal to be a shining light in a dark culture. Once you are settled and established in your marriage, throw open the doors of your home and share with others the life and hope and peace that God has given you (ideally, not too much in the first year). Let others see the love of Christ at work in you and through you.

Understanding Each Other

Wouldn't you like to have a dollar for every book about male and female differences that has been sold in the last ten years? You could retire to a beach-front mansion in the Virgin Islands. On second thought, you could probably *buy* the Virgin Islands!

We've got researchers conducting study after study in an attempt to explain why men and women have such a hard time understanding each other. We've got authors scraping the Milky Way to find metaphors (*Men Are from Mars, Women Are from Venus*) to explain the "battle of the sexes." We've got marital counseling offices filled with frustrated couples who can't seem to connect.

In one sense, this phenomenon is complicated and mysterious. On another level, it's really not that hard to grasp. Take Tiffany and Blake, for example. They're engaged to be married this coming summer. Right now, they're starry-eyed, have racing hormones, and are prone to shove little irritations under the rug. In short, they're in dreamland. They don't have a clue about the reality of married life.

Don't you suppose it would be helpful for them to get a little *premarital* counseling? Imagine the problems they might avoid (or at least be able to take in stride) if they just were forced *in advance* to wrestle with some real issues that lurk just ahead.

At the very least, Tiffany and Blake would, in the hands of a wise and competent counselor, be forced to take a long, hard look at their numerous *differences*. This, by itself, would greatly lessen any shocks or surprises. It would bring their expectations back down to reality. Consider that Tiffany and Blake (like every couple) face the prospect of most (or all) of the following differences:

TOP TEN REASONS FOR PREMARITAL COUNSELING

10. Presentation of biblical truth
9. Honest dialogue about all pertinent issues
8. Forum for asking any question
7. Equipping for long-term success
6. Revealing of expectations
5. Bursting of bubbles
4. Motivation to keep working at your marriage
3. Strengthening of good relationships
2. Dissolution of unhealthy relationships
1. Challenge to put Christ first

- *Different genders:* She's female; he's male. That sexual identity is not a superficial thing; it goes to the core of who they are, and it establishes huge, monumental, gargantuan, gigantic, colossal, profound distinctions between a husband and wife. . .um, suffice it to say the male/female difference is big.
- *Different genes:* He's a unique masterpiece; she's a one-of-a-kind original. They think they are "so much alike." Reality check: no sweethearts/spouses are ever "two peas in a pod."
- *Different backgrounds:* His and her upbringings were different— socially, economically, culturally, geographically, etc.
- *Different personality types:* Beware! He is a quiet, detail-oriented "beaver"-type person; she is a loud, carefree, sloppy, life-of-the-party type of person.

- *Different ways of communicating:* Her verbosity gets on his nerves; his quiet introspection makes her feel shut out!
- *Different ways of thinking:* She thinks globally; he is able to compartmentalize. She is more intuitive and touchy-feely; he is more factual and rational.
- *Different strengths:* He's great with money; she's a disaster, a bankruptcy waiting to happen!
- *Different weaknesses:* She goes to pieces in a conflict situation; he, on the other hand, goes for the throat!
- *Different struggles:* He wrestles with self-image problems; she is brimming with confidence and can't understand "what his deal is!"
- *Different emotions:* At any given moment, he's feeling one way, she another; and for added fun, they have different ways of expressing emotion. She cries at the drop of a hat, at Ragu commercials, for goodness' sake! He last cried in about 2005.
- *Different values:* He would secretly like to throw the TV out into the street; she watches at least three hours a day.
- *Different styles:* She's got a closet full of name-brand clothes and gets her hair cut in a swanky salon; he goes to Arnie the barber and, if asked, would probably guess that J. Crew and Tommy Hilfiger are some kind of rappers or singers.
- *Different convictions:* He thinks drinking is sinful; she likes an occasional glass of wine and fervently believes it's no big deal.
- *Different desires:* He thinks one day he'd like to serve as a missionary in South America; she has no *knowledge* of this, and more importantly no—that's zero, nada, zilch—*desire* for this.
- *Different expectations:* She's expecting a husband who will earn as much as her dad and provide her with a comparable lifestyle; he's, unfortunately, a schoolteacher.
- *Different experiences:* She was molested as a child; he can't understand what this was like or how it has deeply affected her. As he brilliantly observes: "Hey, what's the big deal? It happened almost *twenty years* ago!"

- *Different interests:* He likes to golf...*a lot*; she hates golf because her dad was on the course way too much as she was growing up.

Play marriage counselor, reader. What do you anticipate lies ahead for this love-struck couple?

Suffice it to say the differences between any man and any women are so stark, is it any wonder that couples sigh, shake or scratch their heads, and/or clash with each other? Maybe the most amazing thing of all is that men and women, given all these differences, would EVER be able to live together in peace and joy! Opposites may initially attract, but in time, those wildly different attributes can drive them up the wall.

HEAVEN AND EARTH

"Good marriages might be made in heaven, but they have to be lived out on earth!"

—Unknown

Given the differences between us and our mates, what can we do? Four things:

1. Recognize the differences.

If you don't already, wake up. Go back and reread the last couple of pages.

2. Work to understand the differences.

We never will fully, but we ought to keep trying till the day we die. Instead of viewing him or her as irritating and weird, try to look upon your spouse as fascinating and intriguing. Make it your lifetime assignment to try to figure out what makes that person tick.

3. Learn to appreciate the differences.

Life sure would be simpler (and less surprising) if your spouse thought, felt, acted, and reacted just like you, but it would also be dreadfully dull. Imagine if all ice cream were vanilla (and only vanilla). Think of it this way: if you were exactly alike, one of you would be unnecessary!

4. Utilize the differences.

The truth is, couples are designed by God and sovereignly brought together to complement each other. We need each other. Remember that great line from the first *Rocky* movie where the marble-mouthed boxer tells his sweetheart, the gangly, shy Adrian: "I got gaps; you got gaps. Together we fill gaps"?

That's a *great* description of a healthy married couple. Instead of complaining about the differences and firing verbal bullets at each other because of them, wise couples pull together as one, taking advantage of their God-given uniqueness.

Building Up Your Spouse

Several years back, someone coined the phrase "toxic relationship." The idea behind this phrase is that when you have a marriage where acidic words and hateful actions are the rule, the result is a sick union made up of hurting partners.

 BEWARE THE POWER OF THE TONGUE!

"The words of the reckless pierce like swords, but the tongue of the wise brings healing."

Proverbs 12:18

"The tongue has the power of life and death, and those who love it will eat its fruit."

Proverbs 18:21

"The tongue. . .is a restless evil, full of deadly poison."

James 3:8

Here are some not-too-terribly-edifying practices:

- Teasing too hard ("What's the burnt offering for tonight, dear?")
- Publicly ridiculing your spouse ("She's not a cook, she's an arsonist!")
- Failing to adequately express appreciation (He surprises you with flowers, and you mumble a flat "Thanks.")
- Making light of his/her struggles or feelings ("Gee whiz! I don't see what the big deal is. It's been a whole week since your mom died. Get over it already!")
- Violating a confidence ("Aw, he thinks he's getting fat! I told him he might be a little chubby, but he's definitely not fat. Don't you agree?")
- Not listening
- Forgetting important events (anniversaries, birthdays, etc.)
- Failing to notice big changes (a short haircut, the loss of some weight, the attempt to stop smoking, etc.)

Rather than wounding and damaging each other with harsh words and cruel actions, the New Testament commands: "Therefore encourage one another and build each other up" (1 Thessalonians 5:11).

The Greek verb translated "encourage" actually comes from two words that mean "to call alongside." Basically the idea is strongly coming alongside someone to offer help and support.

The Greek word translated "build. . .up" was a construction term borrowed by the apostle Paul and given a spiritual twist—to strengthen the faith of another, to help them construct a meaningful, healthy relationship with God.

If this is how people are to treat each other in the church, surely we must expect no less in the context of marriage.

It's a clear choice: In the way we look at, speak to, and treat our spouses, we can employ negative, critical, or harsh words and actions. This will, in effect, serve to "destruct" the relationship, chipping away at it, weakening it. Or we can choose to speak and act with gentleness, filled with a desire to encourage and build up our mates.

Having a Support Group
(FRIENDS, FAMILY)

Christian marriage, even under the most ideal circumstances, is a tough proposition.

Consider:

- *It's made up of two sinful people.* Granted, if both parties are believers in Jesus, they're Christians, but they're not perfect. Old habits and selfish, stubborn tendencies still abound! Followers of Christ don't always make Jesus proud. Truth be told, even Christians have been known to hurl Tupperware containers at each other.

- *It's lived out in a hostile, fallen world.* This means trials will come. Hard times will hit unexpectedly. Even godly couples face terrible tragedy and great temptations.

- *It's the target of a diabolical enemy.* If Christian marriage is intended by God to bring honor to Him, and to remind the world of His great love, we can be sure that Satan hates it and does everything within his power to attack and undermine it. Remember how Jesus described the devil? He is a "murderer" (John 8:44) who comes to "kill and destroy" (John 10:10). The sobering truth is that he would *love* to wreck your marriage.

So what can we do? Where can we turn? How about a support group?

We've got support groups for everything from alcoholics to shopaholics, from parents of ADD kids to grieving pet owners. Why not a support group for married couples? It can be an official group, perhaps even one that you form yourself with other couples your age, or in your neighborhood. Or it can be an informal arrangement. For instance, you might meet regularly with:

1. Married friends who love Christ.
You could go out to dinner once a month and talk honestly about your marital successes and failures.

2. An older couple with a healthy marriage.
Perhaps there's a couple in your church who have weathered lots of storms together. Their marriage is strong and proof that it's possible to go the distance and to be much more in love at age sixty-five than at age twenty-five. Strike up a relationship. Find out how they do it. Let them mentor you in the art of marriage.

3. A church.
Ideally, you're official members of a local church, and you're plugged in. People there know you and you know them. You're attending services and sitting under the teaching of God's Word, which is able to strengthen you. You're serving, using the gifts God has given you, thereby growing in the faith and helping build others up. Active church involvement (not just participation in activities, but deep involvement in the lives of your fellow church members) can serve as a kind of safety net for your marriage.

4. A small group.

Most churches nowadays have some form of small-group ministry or Sunday school where you can get together with others and talk about applying the Bible to everyday life. It's common now for many small groups to even sponsor special Bible studies on the various aspects of marriage. What a great forum in which to wrestle with marital problems and hammer out workable solutions.

5. An accountability group.

This is an arrangement (usually men only or women only) in which you meet regularly and ask each other hard questions about how you're doing. It's not a "grill session," but a time for transparency and honesty, a time to find and give encouragement, support, challenge, and help, a time for praying together for each other. If your church doesn't offer such groups, you can start your own with one or two close, trusted friends.

3

KEEPING LOVE ALIVE

Why Is This Important?

A GOOD MARRIAGE ALWAYS BEATS A BAD ONE

It's important to keep love alive in your marriage, if for no other reason than a warm, vibrant relationship beats a cold, dead one. We have a saying: "There are *good* relationships, and there are *bad* relationships; *good ones are better.*"

And you can quote us on that one.

A GOOD MARRIAGE TAKES WORK

Something about dating—the thrill of the chase, the excitement of trying to woo another—typically brings out the best in people. A lot of effort, money, makeup, and cologne go into the all-out attempt to capture the heart of that special "someone."

But then, once the deal is sealed, the carefully groomed guy slowly morphs into a slob. The thoughtful gal no longer does those sweet little "extras." The couple who used to stay up all night talking nonstop now grunt at each other—*if* they speak at all.

What happened?

The couple stopped working at their relationship.

"Working?! You mean I have to go to work to earn a living, and then I have to come home and *keep working*...on my marriage?!"

You got it! Good marriages take work. Like a finely tuned sports car, they need constant monitoring, regular upkeep, and frequent upgrades.

 LOVE IS...

"I believe it was William Shakespeare, or possibly Howard Cosell, who first observed that marriage is very much like a birthday candle, in that the flames of passion burn brightest when the wick of intimacy is first ignited by the disposable butane lighter of physical attraction, but sooner or later the heat of familiarity causes the wax of boredom to drip all over the vanilla frosting of novelty and the shredded coconut of romance.

"I could not have phrased it better myself."

—Dave Barry

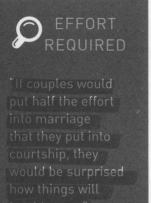
GOOD MARRIAGES MATTER!

The word *mediocre* comes from two Latin words, *media* (meaning "in the middle of") and *ocris* (meaning "mountain"). Perhaps the picture is of a mountain climber who, rather than pushing his way to the summit, decides to end his trek halfway up the mountain. He never finishes. He gets lazy and complacently settles for mediocrity.

This is an accurate, but sad, picture of so many Christian marriages. The individuals quit pursuing intimacy and settle for a comfortable, blah coexistence. "Well, at least we're not like all those couples at the base of the mountain!" they rationalize. But the other perspective is "Yeah, but you also aren't anywhere close to what you could be if you kept climbing."

Why is this such a huge deal? At least three reasons:

- *The glory of God is at stake!* Remember, according to Ephesians 5, marriage is intended to serve as a living picture of the kind of intimate relationship God wants to have with His creatures. If our marriages are dull or cold, then what does that communicate to unbelievers about our God?

- *The future of our society is at stake.* Like it or not, we are being watched, especially by our own children. What kind of advertisement are we for Christian marriage? Do we project an exciting image of warmth and fun and joy? Or do they, because of us, see marriage as a formal living arrangement to be merely endured?

- *Your own happiness is at stake!* Why settle? If there are some simple things you can do to put some sizzle back into your marriage, doesn't it make sense to do them? Who would choose canned meat when he/she could have rib eye?

Having Fun

Would you like to have more fun in your marriage? Then you need to work at being a fun person.

FOR THE RECORD, FUN PEOPLE. . .

Don't take life too seriously.

Yeah, there's a lot of affliction and grief out there, plenty of reasons to be somber. But the Bible speaks a great deal about joy and laughter, too. God has a sense of humor. If you don't believe this, look at just two of His more bizarre creatures: the duckbill platypus and the television evangelist.

Don't take themselves too seriously.

Lighten up. Get loose. To paraphrase the former Israeli prime minister Golda Meir, "Don't be so serious, you're not that great!"

Laugh at themselves.

You might as well—others are! (If not to your face, then behind your back.) So what if you dump an entire bowl of vichyssoise in your lap. It's not the end of the world (though maybe the end of that pair of trousers).

Look for the offbeat and quirky in everyday situations and/or responsibilities.

"Fun" is a state of mind. It's a way of thinking. If you don't take life too seriously, almost any experience can bring about laughter and fun. Instead of getting impatient standing in a long line at the driver's license bureau, why not watch people and get a kick out of the lady behind the desk who's acting like Barney Fife?

Regularly use and develop their sense of humor.

Read the comics, watch clean comedians. You may never be a Robin Williams, but you can laugh and learn to make others laugh. In short, you can be a person who is really fun to be with (and that can REALLY enhance a marriage!).

You don't need a lot of money:

- Try out a new recipe. The fun here is in working together and striving to create something that is deliciously wonderful. You get to sample the fruit of your labors, and either you'll savor how wonderful it is (*that's* fun), or you'll get to joke about how dreadful it turned out (that's funny. . .in a depressing sort of way).

- Perfect an inexpensive, delicious homemade pizza recipe. Here the fun is in knowing that, for $4.12 you can now enjoy the same meal you've previously been paying $15.39 to enjoy.

- Make up silly games. For example, on the living room floor take turns trying to toss a crumpled piece of paper into each other's empty glass. Contests like this provide hours of spellbinding entertainment.

- Do a puzzle. See which person can put the most pieces together. Brag about it. Tease (but not too hard!).

- Watch the Home Shopping Channel or a really bad infomercial. You've never heard such ridiculous commentary in all your life!

- Look back over scrapbooks. Smile over old memories. Chuckle at bad haircuts. Chortle at hideous fashions. Guffaw at. . .never mind.

- Borrow movies from the library (comedies like the Marx Brothers, the "Road" movies starring Bob Hope and Bing Crosby, or old Jerry Lewis classics).

- Make a clay pot together. (If you don't think *this* is fun, you never saw the movie *Ghost*!)

- Go to the museum. Laugh at some of the objects and paintings that are considered "art." Watch the serious art patrons, how they study each exhibit.

- Go camping. Spiders, snakes, trying to sleep on the hard ground, eating gritty food—hey, it just doesn't get much more fun than this!

Seriously, if you're a good sport, you can find a lot of humor in a wilderness adventure like this. And you get funny memories you'll relive for years to come.

- People-watch at the park or mall. Smile at the quirks and idiosyncrasies of God's beloved creatures.
- Share a hobby together. Go bird-watching or do crafts. Take up painting.
- Go garage-saling. Now THERE'S an interesting subculture. It's great fun to watch what people will clamor for and fight over. And often you can find some incredible bargains.
- Exercise (walk, jog, bike, play tennis, etc.) together.
- Take an offbeat vacation. Go with no agenda, or if you're really brave, no clear destination. Just drive and be laid back. Go with the flow. See what happens. Trust God to lead you into something or someplace fascinating.
- Visit a nearby attraction that you've never seen. It's said that familiarity breeds contempt, but proximity does, too! Why is it that most New Yorkers have never been to the Statue of Liberty? Don't succumb to this phenomenon. Check things out. Get the spouse and the kids and drive to the closest state park. Pay a visit to Irving's House of Reptiles over on Highway 367.
- Rollerblade. It's fun if you're good at it. It's hilarious if you're not. (Always use safety equipment, since trips to the ER are NOT fun!)
- Take a dance class. Classic or country-western, you'll laugh a lot as you try to get your four left feet to jitterbug or two-step in concert. (Plus you get to put your hands on each other!)

(!) MEMORIES

"On a lark my wife and I once went to a free poetry reading at a small bookstore. It was one of the funniest things we've ever witnessed.

"Bohemian types playing bongos, timid-looking businessmen dramatically yelling out bizarre rhymes to musical accompaniment—we nearly wet our pants. That was twelve years ago, and we still smile when we talk about that rich memory."

—Walter, Dallas, Texas

THE JOY OF SEX

Sex can make *any day* fun.
Sex can make *any place* fun.
Do we need to spell this out?
Okay, for all you really "unfun" people. . .

- *Fun in the kitchen.* Cook a meal together. Then take off all your clothes and spray each other with whipped cream. (Best not to do this during the supper hour when the kids are present.)
- *Fun in the living room.* Build a fire and make love in front of the fireplace. (Not recommended in the months May–August).
- *Fun in the yard.* Relax! Not actually out IN the yard. Rather, tidy up the lawn and garden. Or plant some vegetable or flower seeds. Talk "dirty" to each other (pun intended). Then come in and take a shower together!
- *Fun in the bathroom.* Take a bubble bath together.
- *Fun in the bedroom.* Scented candles, lingerie, cologne, romantic music. . .you get the picture. Or play an adult version of an old familiar game: "*Strip* Boggle" or "*Strip* Yahtzee" (i.e., each time you lose, you forfeit an article of clothing). Somehow, playing these games as a kid was never so much fun!

FUN PEOPLE

Having a "fun" marriage takes a real commitment. We need to be fun people first (filled with the joy of the Lord and sheer wonder at God's marvelous gift of life). We also need to be willing to work at finding the hilarity in common moments. Happiness IS a choice. So opt daily to be a "joyful, fun Christian" and not a "sourpuss saint."

Date Your Mate

It is possible to be too young to date, but there is no such thing as being too old to date. In fact, the best marriages are that way, at least in part, because the couple keep working at their marriage. They fight complacency. They resist the "rut" tendency. They plan and pull off creative ways to have fun together. In short, they never stop dating.

MARITAL DATING YIELDS LOTS OF RICH, GOD-HONORING RESULTS:

- Extended time together to deepen your relationship
- An opportunity for uninterrupted communication (sharing and listening)
- A means of making (and keeping) one's marriage a priority
- Giving harried parents/spouses a fun break from their hectic lives
- An example of love and commitment for the children and the neighbors (in an era when the institution of marriage is a laughingstock)
- A chance for replenishment—emotionally, spiritually, mentally

WHAT CONSTITUTES A DATE?

A date implies a special effort to be together with the goal of doing something fun and out of the ordinary.

Note:

It must be *special*.

It should take some *effort*.

It has to be *together*.

The goal is *fun* and relaxation. You ought to come home replenished and renewed from your time together.

The quality of being *out of the ordinary* sets it apart and makes it memorable.

IS DATING BIBLICAL?

There is no command in 1 Hesitations or 2 Hezekiah that reads: "Husband, stayest at home with thy wife? Stay not! Go ye together on a date!" In short, the only kind of dates you find in the Bible are the kind you eat.

THESE ARE NOT TECHNICALLY "DATES":

Attending church

Going to vote

Doing errands together

Grocery shopping

Going to separate movies that happen to be showing simultaneously at the same movieplex

Getting the oil changed together

Mowing the grass together

Sitting in the living room together (she's clipping coupons; he's watching the new special *America's Worst Golfing Disasters*)

Going to your child's athletic event together

TEN IMPORTANT MARITAL DATING FACTS/TIPS

1. If you don't make dating a priority, it won't happen.
2. A formal invitation makes any date more special. (For example call from the office or leave a note like *"Hey, beautiful, I'd like to take you to dinner on Friday night at seven. Interested?"*)
3. Couples need to date on a regular basis (not once in a blue moon).
4. Spending large sums of money is not necessary.
5. Having children does NOT mean an end to your dating career (see "Finding Quality Child Care" on page 49).
6. The husband needs to take the lead in dating. (Note: Guys, you get no "dating credits" if your wife initiates and does all the planning of an evening out.)
7. Creativity is crucial. (Going to dinner and/or a movie should be the dating exception rather than the rule—a potted plant could pull that off! Do something wild. Take her dancing. Spring for a carriage ride through the streets of downtown.)
8. If either spouse has to ask at the end of the evening, "Was *this* supposed to be a *date*?" rest assured it probably wasn't legitimate.
9. Guys, if you start taking your wife on regular dates, she will love

you. Your married male friends, on the other hand, will want to give you a wedgie.

10. Good dating generally leads to good relating, which can often lead to good "mating" (if you catch our drift).

FINDING QUALITY CHILD CARE

- Grandparents in the area
- Surrogate grandparents (from church or the neighborhood)
- Parents who live nearby
- Grown siblings who are trustworthy (we're not talking your ditzy sister "Seabreeze" who lives at the beach and sells paintings of seagulls out of her van)
- Christian collegiates (they will often swap child care for the chance to wash clothes and scrounge a meal from your pantry)
- Respected high schoolers with a reputation for being highly competent and responsible
- Friends (take turns watching each other's children; e.g., the Crumpleys watch your kids on Wednesday nights; you watch theirs on Thursday)
- Young married couples in your church (these are often good candidates for weekends away…they can provide child care, bring in the mail, and feed the pets)

WHY POSTMARITAL DATING IS BETTER THAN PREMARITAL DATING

Premarital Dating	Postmarital Dating
Nervousness	No reason to be nervous
A blunder is a disaster!	Blunders happen all the time!
Don't know each other well	Know each other intimately
Small talk; chitchat	Meaningful conversation
Worried if he/she likes you	Relax—he/she MARRIED you!
Have to go home separately	Get to go home together
Will there be another date?	There WILL be another date!
Evening might end with a kiss	Evening might end in *bliss!*

CREATIVE DATING IDEAS:

- You can get many movie scripts right off the Internet. Act out your favorite scenes. Videotape yourselves doing your best Harrison Ford or Meg Ryan impressions, than laugh your heads off.
- Go to the symphony (sometimes they even offer free performances).
- Take advantage of drama productions at nearby high schools or colleges. The cost is generally low, and you may catch a rising star.
- On a cold night, find a restaurant with a fireplace and try to get a table up close.
- Eat at a new restaurant in town.
- Attend a Shakespeare festival and watch a play by the bard.
- Borrow a telescope, drive to the country, and look at constellations.
- Lie on the ground on a clear night and watch for shooting stars.
- Go sailing (small sailboat, small lake) in the late afternoon—just the two of you.
- Talk a walk down the beach at sunset.
- Go feed the ducks in a peaceful park.
- "Listen up!" night. Drive around and try to see how many distinct sounds you can identify. See who has the best auditory organs.
- Check out a nearby antique store or two. There's no telling what kind of treasure you might find.
- Determine which night of the week your library stays open late. Go explore and hang out together.
- Visit a museum. This can be a cultural feast.
- Borrow a neighbor's puppy or kitten for the evening, and let it amuse you.
- Buy a snack, sit on a bench, and do some people-watching at the mall. Play the game where you find people who resemble famous celebrities. Study people and try to guess what their backgrounds/stories are.
- Go watch Little League ball games. Unlike the pampered pros (many of whom are head cases and prima donnas), these little tykes play for the sheer joy of it. You'll laugh your head off, and watching the parents is an eye-opening experience.

- Explore a nearby warehouse discount store (e.g., Sam's) around meal-time. You'll get to sample all kinds of free food.
- Surf the net together. If you already have access, this won't cost you a penny.
- Together, do a random act of kindness for someone. Mow an elderly neighbor's lawn. Run some errands for a sick friend. Provide free baby-sitting for those new parents who need to get out. Clean out a closet and donate those old clothes/items to the Salvation Army or Goodwill.
- Do something constructive together. Wash and vacuum your car(s). Do homework. Work on some creative Christmas gifts so that you're ready when the holidays arrive.
- Play Ping-Pong.
- Go shoot pool.
- Hit a bucket of golf balls at the driving range.
- Play goofy golf.
- Do a project together. Have a garage sale with another couple. Paint a classroom at the church.
- Go to a farmer's market.
- Go pick (name a fruit) together.
- Window-shop at the mall. (Begin your spree with an imaginary $10,000 each. Write down what you'd buy.)
- Get one of those "Special Saver" coupon books from a school or civic group that is doing fund-raising. Though the initial cost might be thirty dollars, you'll end up with all kinds of great discounts and two-for-one offers, and the coupons don't usually expire for a whole year.
- Get in a Jacuzzi together. Let your troubles melt away.
- Rendezvous at a local hotel for a passionate evening of lovemaking.
- Give him/her homemade coupons for
  a massage.
  a home-cooked gourmet meal.
  a trip to the frozen yogurt stand.

DINNER BELL

"After a good dinner one can forgive anybody, even one's own relations."
—Oscar Wilde

Think of the millions of husbands and wives who carefully monitor their mutual funds, frantically keep up their cars, and feverishly work on improving their homes, golf swings, figures, etc.

Question: Why do so few of these same couples take the time or make even a minimal effort to keep their marriages alive and exciting?

Romantic Movies:

An Affair to Remember
While You Were Sleeping
Sleepless in Seattle
The Princess Bride
It Happened One Night
Sabrina
Breakfast at Tiffany's

Not-So-Romantic Movies:

Night of the Living Dead
Saving Private Ryan
The Terminator
Rocky V
Animal House
Attack of the Killer Tomatoes
Armageddon

Gifts

What better way to express your love than by giving your sweetheart a gift? What more tangible way to demonstrate thoughtfulness and sacrifice? What better way keeps the economy humming and the stock market going up?

HINTS FOR GIFT-GIVING SUCCESS:

Pick your occasions. At a minimum, you ought to give gifts on his/her birthday, your anniversary, Valentine's Day, and Christmas.

If you're REALLY into this, you can expand your generosity to include the anniversary of your first date/first kiss/engagement/first stomach virus together, Groundhog Day, National Cauliflower Week, etc.

DATING DISASTER

If the goal of marital dating is to have fun and put a little spark back into the old relationship, you might want to avoid mood-killing statements like these:

"Is it just me, or does that dress make you look larger than you are?"

"How about dropping me off at the mall, and then you could go on and finish the date by yourself?"

"Dinner? Tonight?! And miss *Matlock*!? Why in the world would we want to do that?"

"You are SO sweet! My favorite restaurant! Um, would you mind if we got separate tables?"

"That sounds like a fun evening, but to tell you the truth, I'd rather you just gave me the cash you were planning to spend."

"Go on a date? Heh, heh. You're kidding, right? With YOU?! Ha, ha, ha. AH, HA HA HA HA!"

Plan ahead. Most of us are not exactly wired to think far into the future. Guys, especially, tend to follow the Omigosh-it's-our-anniversary-I-need-to-run-to-Walmart-before-it-closes! approach. This last-minute strategy typically results in not-so-endearing gifts like the Oster corn and callus remover.

However, by setting aside an hour or two, say, at the beginning of the year, you can list out all the upcoming, important gift-giving dates and begin to jot down creative ideas for presents. Also, this advance planning gives you the opportunity to begin saving for more expensive items, like the Oster corn and callus remover, deluxe edition—*now for women with really large feet.*

Pay attention. Listen as he/she offhandedly mentions needed or desired objects. It's an established fact that spouses often give subtle clues like. . .

(Him): "I'd like to take this sorry watch and beat the springs out of it with a sledgehammer."

(Her): "You know, if I ever did have another birthday, like say, next Thursday, and if my sweet mate decided he wanted to get me something I would really adore, I'd ask for a new watch, maybe even the Timex® Encuricom, model #25789, on sale now at Sears for only $49.97."

Give it the "extra" touch. Don't just fold the store bag over and staple it shut. Wrap it up in nice paper with an elegant bow. Don't just walk up and say, "Here, this is for you!" Leave a note, telling him/her where to find the gift. Use a little gift-giving "foreplay" to make the experience more fun and interesting.

Homemade is good. You could go out and pay $1,500 for that new armoire she saw in the window of Harrison's Furniture downtown, or, by golly, you could go purchase $400 worth of lumber and $2,890 worth of power tools (but, hey, you'd have them for future projects!) and whip that thing out yourself. It's the thought that counts, right? Think of it—how much more it would mean to her if you accidentally sawed off your left pinky trying to give her what her heart craves!

Seriously, consider your beloved's interests and tastes. Plan ahead. Then MAKE your own present—a framed picture, a hand carving, a needle-point wall hanging, etc. It sounds corny, but this is the kind of personalized gift that ends up being a treasured possession.

Unexpected is good. It's one thing to give gifts and cards on the days when the mall merchants and Hallmark say you should. It's a higher kind of love that gives a gift for no special occasion—"just because you're the greatest wife/husband in the world."

Personal is good. Tailoring the gift to your spouse (his/her unique personality) is a way to communicate thoughtfulness. Don't just buy him a dozen golf balls. Have his name engraved on them. That way, all his buddies at the club can have a good laugh when they find six of his shots along the edges of the water hazard on hole #9.

MEMORABLE BIBLE GIFTS

- As a dowry for Saul's daughter, David gave the unusual (and not exactly practical!) "gift" of two hundred Philistine foreskins (1 Samuel 18:27).
- In an attempt to pacify Joseph, the sons of Jacob gave their unrecognized brother "a little balm and a little honey, some spices and myrrh, some pistachio nuts and almonds" (Genesis 43:11).
- Pharaoh gave his daughter the conquered city of Gezer (1 Kings 9:16).
- The Queen of Sheba gave King Solomon "120 talents of gold, large quantities of spices, and precious stones" (1 Kings 10:10).
- The magi brought the baby Jesus "gifts of gold, frankincense and myrrh" (Matthew 2:11).

THINK AHEAD

Guys, you can be a hero, a "knight in shining armor," possibly even "Husband of the Year" if you just make it obvious to your wife that you've been thinking of and planning for this gift for some time. Such thoughtfulness is rare among men, and it is absolutely treasured by women.

How to Be Romantic

Most women have a genetic advantage when it comes to romance. They weep at movies like *An Affair to Remember*. They enjoy going to weddings, and they actually pay attention. They can tell you ten years later what color dresses the bridesmaids wore.

Guys don't get it. Most males have overactive sex hormones and under-developed romance genes. The result is that if romance is what men have to "do" for a romp in the proverbial hay, then what's a few flowers (and maybe even a box of chocolate) every year or so? Listen up: There's a *lot* more to romance than that.

Men, if you are romantically challenged, the best advice we can give is for you to visit the "classic/oldies" section of your video store and watch a different Cary Grant movie every week for the next two months.

Note: Sylvester Stallone and Clint Eastwood movies are not recommended.

ROMANCE VERSUS SEX

Romance is more comprehensive than sex. Romance seeks to touch the heart and the emotions (and not just the genitalia!). Romance is subtle, playful. It delights not merely in the body, but in the mind, the personality. Romance is a mind-set, an around-the-clock phenomenon. It flirts, it teases. You can be romantic anywhere, anytime. You can't do that with sex (at least and stay out of jail!). You can have romance without sex (fun). You can also have sex without romance (not so fun). However, it is a well-established fact that the happiest and healthiest couples strive to be romantic, and this typically leads to a more fulfilling sexual relationship.

SIMPLE WAYS TO BE ROMANTIC:

Shower. (Being dirty and smelly/having body odor is *not* romantic!)

Wear perfume/cologne.

Dress nicely. (Don't be a slob!)

Floss and brush. (As a wise old dentist once said, "Be true to your teeth, and they'll never be false to you!")

Keep a supply of breath mints, gum, and mouthwash handy.

Hold hands as much as possible.

Whisper "sweet nothings" in each other's ears.

Leave little love notes around the house, in lunch bags, in cars, in purses.

Call for no reason.

Exercise (and lose those unwanted pounds).

Eat healthily (so that you don't become overweight).

Pray that God would help you be less self-centered and more thoughtful.

Kiss a lot (and not always just as a prelude to sex).

Share your deepest desires and dreams.

Be spontaneous.

Put the kids down early, and eat supper late.

Invest in one of those "Romantic Love Songs" CDs.

Buy and burn some scented candles.

Stare into each other's eyes.

Stare into a fire together.

Share a blanket on the couch on a cold night.

Sit side by side on the couch.

Caress his/her scalp.

Wink at each other.

Give each other "the look."

Hug.

 WISE MEN SAY

If you want a crash course in romantic love, read the Song of Solomon. In fact, read it aloud to your spouse. The king of Israel and his beloved enjoyed an unabashedly sexy, romantic, erotic, sensual relationship.

Anyone who says the Bible was written by prudes and for prudes has never read this book!

Feed each other (fondue, for some reason, is especially romantic).

Reminisce about your courtship.

Nibble on his/her earlobes.

Men: Give a back rub with no hidden motives, no strings attached (i.e., no intercourse expected).

Women: Invest in some hot lingerie. Put it on, so your husband can take it off!

ALL COMES DOWN TO THIS

The essence of romance is thinking of the other person: his/her needs, wants, desires. When you delight in your mate and seek to put him/her first, your marriage takes on a romantic feel. Each spouse feels cared for, special, valued, and cherished. The result is fireworks—of a good kind!

4

HAVING A
HEALTHY HOME

Dividing Chores

"Mrs. Hunter, you are charged with assault, specifically, hurling a large fruit-cake at your husband because he refused to help you clean up the house after a neighborhood Christmas party. How do you plead?"

"I'm guilty, Your Honor. . .but if I may address the court, I charge HIM with NEVER LIFTING A FINGER TO HELP AROUND THE HOUSE! You lazy jerk, you selfish CREEP!"

BAM! BAM! BAM! "Order! Order in the court!"

Situations like this happen thousands of times a day, if not in the court-rooms of our fair land, then at least in the minds of disgruntled spouses who just want a little help around the house doing everyday tasks.

Running a household takes a tremendous amount of work. Numerous chores have to be completed at regular intervals or a simple three-bedroom home can quickly resemble New York City in the midst of a sanitation strike.

WORK TOGETHER

Whenever possible, work together. For example, one cooks and another washes pots and dishes. One vacuums the car, while the other wipes it out and does the windows. This kind of cooperation builds unity. Also it takes into account the old adage "Misery loves company."

When it comes to completing chores, here are the options:

(Wives are hereby warned not to read item one while attempting to swallow.)

1. The husband does them all.
2. The wife does them all (a plan favored by most men).
3. A brigade of butlers (led by a British chap named Chesterton) and a platoon of maids (all named Cozette) do them all.
4. The husband and wife split them up. (Most modern couples not living at the Hamptons, and without the last name Gates or Spielberg, have to settle for this option.)

How to divide up the chores

A number of innovative methods for divvying up household tasks have been employed by creative couples:

- "Eeney, meeney, miney. . ."
- "If we ignore it another month, do you think the neighbors will do it?"
- Consult the biblical Urim and Thummim (or flipping a coin).
- Make your sullen teenagers do it (at the threat of not getting to borrow the car).
- He: "You do all the inside stuff; I'll take care of the lawn and garden." She: "We live in an apartment!"

 SHARE THE LOAD

The Bible tells husbands to love their wives as Christ loves his church (Ephesians 5). Somehow it's hard to square this command with the husband who kicks back in his easy chair to watch *Most Horrendous Construction Deaths Caught on Video* while his exhausted wife is working nonstop from 5:00–10:00 p.m. cooking, doing laundry, washing the dishes, and getting the kids ready for bed.

There is a healthier way to divide the labor

Have a "draft" where you list out everything that needs to be done, and you take turns selecting preferred jobs.

Once you're done with items like sweeping, mopping, dusting, etc., usually there are at least two jobs left that no one in their right mind would ever naturally want to do. At that point you have to use Solomonic wisdom to broker an agreement that all can live with: "All right, I'll clean the dog droppings out of the yard while you clean the upchuck out of the infant seat."

Expectations

Newlyweds Muffy and Biff Baxter are severely disenchanted after their honeymoon trip to La Promenade, a fancy French restaurant. Why? For the same reason Arnelle and Keyshawn Thompson are majorly disappointed with their new car.

Unmet expectations.

The Baxters were expecting a romantic evening with exquisitely prepared food and unparalleled service. They ended up paying through the nose for something that tasted like a home economics project, served by a college kid with an attitude.

By buying the Plynda Omelette, *Motor Trend's* Car of the Decade, the Thompsons assumed they were saying farewell to all those trips to the auto repair shop. But in the first three months, they've made six trips to the Plynda service department with their bright yellow Omelette.

Four Profound Laws about Expectations:

1. We ALL have them about EVERYTHING (from books to movies, from Saturdays to holidays).
2. The degree to which reality fails to measure up to our expectations is the degree to which we will feel disappointed.
3. Repeated disappointments may lead to disenchantment, despair, or even disgust.
4. These first three laws are *especially* at work in marriage.

A few of the main areas about which married couples have expectations:

Sex	Finances (giving,	Clothes
Vacations	saving, investing)	Pets
Holidays	Roles	Socializing
Use of free time	Spending patterns	Decorating
Exercise	Time with family	Relationship with
Hobbies	Communication	in-laws
Sleep habits	habits/styles	Entertainment
Time apart	Diet	
Children	Shopping	

Marital expectations are generally subconscious and seldom verbalized, so that, for example, he comes into the marriage "assuming" that their annual vacation will consist of two weeks in July lounging at the beach. (After all, this is what his family did every year he can remember.) Meanwhile, she is envisioning three or four "mini-vacations" filled with high-energy shopping and whirlwind sightseeing.

Do you see the potential for disappointment and/or conflict?

What can couples do to minimize the disappointment?
1. Talk about your expectations.

The ideal time to clarify expectations is *before* marriage. It's really helpful to know (prior to saying "I do") that, while your heart is set on five or six kids, your beloved is expecting maybe one (and only if that one can come with a low-maintenance guarantee). However, every couple (even after the fact) is wise to make a list like the one above and work through it together.

2. Compromise.

If she wants to hang the giant cat picture over the living room sofa, but he was expecting a more manly motif—like heads of slain animals, clearly both sides need to give a little. Perhaps a tastefully mounted house cat head? Seriously, stubbornness will get you nowhere. Well, actually, it will get you lots of places. . .they're just not places a married couple need to go.

3. Do away with unrealistic expectations.

If you're both schoolteachers (and thus, like all educators, vastly underpaid), it's probably not realistic to expect that you and your sweetie will be able to spend each summer at your own private villa overlooking the Mediterranean. Be a bit more reasonable. Lower your sights a tad. If you're really careful and creative, you might be able to afford an annual camping trip to some national parks out west.

4. Learn the difference between hoping for something and demanding something.

Example: While at the office Dave catches a whiff of some exotic perfume. Somehow (and scientists are not sure how this happens since this is such a rare phenomenon among men) this scent causes Dave to envision an intimate evening with his wife, Dianne. As he mulls over the prospect in his mind, he moves subtly from "Man, that sure would be romantic!" to "By golly, I'm going for it tonight!" Now Dave has an expectation (perhaps even a demanding spirit). What happens if he gets home and Dianne has a headache?

5. Learn the art of contentment.

Be appreciative for what you've got. Develop an attitude of gratitude. Those with long wish lists tend to be the unhappiest people.

6. Be accepting.

Romans 15:7 encourages us to accept one another, just as Christ has accepted us. It's wise to apply this principle when discussing expectations with your spouse. Yeah, his expectation of "no leftovers ever" is a bit extreme. But so is your expectation that he never be a minute late anywhere.

Seven Things You Need in a Healthy Home

Healthy, happy homes share common traits:

They have at *least* two bathrooms, separate his and her walk-in closets, and are furnished with a late-model, heavy-duty washer and dryer.

Seriously, healthy, happy homes *are* marked by these characteristics:

1. Faith

God spoke through Moses to the ancient Hebrews (and to us!) about the family (not the church) as the primary tool for passing on a strong spiritual heritage:

"You must love the LORD your God with all your heart, all your soul, and all your strength. And you must commit yourselves wholeheartedly to these commands I am giving you today. Repeat them again and again to your children. Talk about them when you are at home and when you are away on a journey, when you are lying down and when you are getting up again" (Deuteronomy 6:5–7 NLT).

If we don't teach our children to love and serve God, we have failed in our most critical role as parents.

What are you doing to pass on a solid biblical faith?

2. Love

The world has redefined love as either a sentimental feeling that comes and goes, a hormonal (read "sexual") urge that demands immediate satisfaction, or a mealymouthed mushiness that permits anything and everything. On the contrary, biblical love, the hallmark of every healthy family, is unconditional, unselfish, courageous, holy, and unwavering. It sets limits and boundaries. It insists on compliance with reasonable standards. True love seeks the best for others (even when that "best" is painful or unpopular).

How does your family love—according to God's standards or the world's?

3. Honesty/Integrity

In a decadent culture where lying is commonly accepted and where integrity is on the endangered list, our families must be bastions of truth. This is foundational! Deception of any kind erodes marriages, homes, and ultimately societies. We must insist on honesty and we must practice what we preach.

Is your family marked by utter truthfulness and trustworthiness?

4. Affirmation/Acceptance

Daily our family members venture out into a cruel and uncertain world. All day long, they/we are beaten up and torn down emotionally. The least we can do is to try to make our homes places of safety and warmth. In *The Language of Love* Gary Smalley and John Trent remind us, "Insecurity in a home pulls our roots; security provides the depth and shelter. . .to survive." Is your home an oasis of love? A place of encouragement? A light in the darkness? Remember, compassion is learned at home.

Do your family members come home to kind words and strong hugs?

5. Forgiveness

A noted psychiatrist once commented that about half the people in the mental institutions in this country could be released if they could only be convinced that they are forgiven! What a tragedy! So many guilty people, so many whose lives are shattered by regret and shame. What better place than the home to learn the twin truths that we all "blow it" and that it is possible, in Christ, both to *be* forgiven and to forgive others who have wronged us. If we believe the Gospel, we do not have to walk around under a cloud of condemnation. And we have no right to condemn others.

Is your family involved in the amazing, life-changing, perpetual project of granting and experiencing God's forgiveness?

6. Tradition

Families in previous eras put down roots. All the grandparents and cousins lived in close proximity, sharing meals and life. Unique traditions were developed and were handed down through the generations. Not anymore. Our fast-paced, transient, impersonal pop culture means the demise of meaningful family rituals.

What kind of traditions are you developing and practicing?

7. Humor

Because life invariably tends toward somberness and seriousness, we need more laughter in our homes. In her book *Getting Out of Your Kids' Faces and into Their Hearts*, Valerie Bell writes: "Shared laughter is like family glue. It is the stuff of family well-being and all-is-well thoughts. It brings us together as few other things can."

When is the last time your family howled and hooted, bent over with joy, tears in the eyes?

The Place of Your Career— Or Should You Have One?

Researchers have concluded that money is a really helpful thing for most married couples and/or families. So, obviously, SOMEONE (either husband or wife, or perhaps both) needs to work and bring home that proverbial bacon.

The question is, should *both* husband and wife pursue a career? If kids aren't in the equation, this is not a difficult issue. As long as both parties have the desire and opportunity to work, and assuming they are in agreement about the details, a two-career marriage can be a wonderful arrangement.

Two incomes can mean a greater ability to give money to eternal causes, a freedom from debt, a chance to make some long-term investments and possibly "retire" early, so that one is freed up to serve God full-time, possibly even overseas.

But what if a couple have children, especially infants and/or preschool-aged children? Here the answers are not always so clear. Couples have to wrestle with assorted child-care questions:

- With whom do we feel comfortable leaving our child(ren)?
- Will we one day regret missing much of their early development?
- What values will our children pick up while in the care of others?
- Will there be long-term negative emotional effects?

- When the rising cost of day care is deducted from that extra paycheck, is it really worth it, from a purely financial standpoint?

More and more new parents are deciding to have one party put his/her career on hold for six or eight years, at least until their children are in school. They recognize that talented people will always be able to land a job, but parents only have a short window of time in which to influence their children. Others are reconfiguring their career responsibilities and finding they are able to work out of their homes. Still others are starting at-home businesses.

What about demanding careers?

It was Peter Lynch, former manager of the Fidelity Magellan Mutual Fund, who once observed that no one, on his or her deathbed, will wish they had spent more time at the office. Some jobs, no matter how prestigious or high paying, are simply not worth the toll they take on a spouse and/or children.

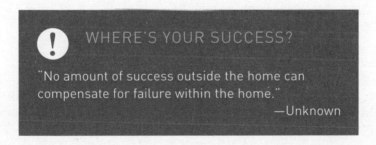

! WHERE'S YOUR SUCCESS?

"No amount of success outside the home can compensate for failure within the home."

—Unknown

5

CHILDREN

Children

CURVES AHEAD

Before children enter the marriage, the couple have a lot of freedom. They run out to the store or spontaneously go to a movie. They visit with friends after church. They go away for a night here and a weekend there. There's little to keep them from being spontaneous and free. Much of that comes to an end with two of the most powerful words in the English language: "I'm pregnant."

When the wife utters those words to her husband for the first time, life as they know it comes to a screeching halt and will never be the same again.

CHANGES COMING

Physical

With pregnancy comes change to both the husband and wife. The wife's body goes through massive changes as her body prepares to make room for the baby. As the baby grows, her body changes. These changes will often cause her to feel fat or unattractive. And don't forget that these changes are physically rough. Even women who are usually energetic are likely to feel run down and tired.

The mistake husbands make is to assume that once the baby is born, all will return to normal. Not always so. Mom's body will take a long time to return to normal, and you'll both be tired after the baby is born. Lastly, there will be even *more* changes if Mom begins nursing.

Emotional

Emotions that were once balanced will go haywire. If the mother-to-be was calm, cool, and collected, she might find herself unpredictable and quick to tears. After the baby is born, the hormones don't bounce back overnight. In fact, the emotional roller coaster gets worse before it gets better. Sometimes women feel more rational during pregnancy than in the first month or so after the child is born. *Expect this change.*

Sexual

Some women have no changes in their sex drive during pregnancy. Others change quite a bit. It's important to talk about what you're feeling and what you're expecting of your partner. The woman's body takes time to return to normal. Some women bounce back quicker than others. Some need more time.

TURN IT UP!

"My wife and I were surprised by the changes that happened to her body. One change that we didn't expect was that she always felt cold. She'd turn up the thermostat during the day. I'd come home and think that I was entering a sauna so I'd turn it down. She'd turn it up in the middle of the night, and I'd wake up in a sweat and turn it back down. Since we never saw each other adjust the temperature, it took us three months before we realized we were fighting each other. Once we figured it out, we were able to compromise."

—Rodney, Grand Rapids, Michigan

Social

This one may take you by surprise. Your conversation with others will take a drastic shift. Before the pregnancy, you talked to others about travel, books you're reading, or the Knicks. Now you'll find yourself talking about nursery colors, childbirth classes, and baby names. Once the baby is born, you'll find that most people talk more about the baby than about you.

Other Changes

There are other changes you'll experience, too. For example, your *budget* will change. Maybe before, you thought nothing of dropping five dollars for a vanilla latte. Now you might need to scrape together your dimes for diapers and wipes. Other expenses like high chairs, cribs, and wallpaper for the baby's room tend to add up quickly.

You may need to move. Do you have enough room for the baby? Babies themselves don't take much space. But once they begin crawling—then walking—you'll realize how much space they take. Couples who once got along fine in a one- or two-bedroom apartment often begin looking around for another place.

TOP TEN LESSONS ABOUT PARENTING A NEWBORN

1. Never jostle a newly fed baby.
2. Always put down a drop cloth before burping a baby.
3. Every new parent should have a battery-operated baby swing.
4. You can lead a baby to bed, but you can't make her sleep.
5. Always be on your guard when changing a baby boy.
6. Babies don't read the same baby-care books that their parents read. And they certainly don't read chapters that say, "By eight weeks your baby should be sleeping through the night."
7. There are few crises to a baby that a mother's arms can't ease.
8. Nurses say that newborn, breast-fed babies have sweet-smelling diapers. That's a lie.
9. Babies manage to become dirty without ever going anywhere.
10. Strangers often hold doors for parents with strollers as well as let them go first in line. Consider bringing a stroller with you everywhere you go—even if your baby isn't with you.

Children: Are They a Bond or a Wedge?

The answer: Yes.

CHILDREN CAN BE A BOND

Children can be a great way to grow together and get to know each other better. Children provide many daily events and crises that can draw parents together. The parents who work together as a team grow closer together. Raising children gives you a common goal that allows you to work together on the most rewarding assignment of your lives.

Develop a Unified Front

Determine your parenting philosophy together. What is most important to you as parents? How do you want your children to turn out? When and how will you discipline your children? Answering questions like these together will help you develop a unified front. Some parents, either formally or informally, come up with a mission statement for parenting. A mission statement is a sentence or two that helps direct your lives as parents. Examples of a good mission statement are

> To teach our children to love God with all their hearts.
> To teach our children to be hard workers for Christ and His
> kingdom.

Developing a mission statement is a good idea. Work *together* to decide what is most important to you.

Set Goals and Plan Together

Who's going to teach your children to read? Who will take them to the zoo? You're not two independent adults working on the same project. Work as a team to set your goals and plans. You'll have many heart-to-heart talks as you decide what's most important to you.

Solve Problems Together

Face it. You'll have good kids—at least you're planning on it. But even the best kids will have problems. Work together to solve the problems as they arise.

As they get older, the practical issues will change. As your children grow, you won't have to worry about them stealing candy from the drugstore, but you'll have a new set of problems. All along the way, the character qualities you're trying to instill will remain the same. Work together to instill integrity and other character traits you want your child to develop throughout his or her life.

 MISSIONARY GRANDPARENTS

Mike and Jill worked together at every aspect of parenting. Their child had a learning disability, so they spent a lot of energy getting their only son through school. Working together throughout their son's childhood, they became a great team. They solved problems and set goals together. They quickly discovered that they worked better together than they did by themselves. Their son grew and successfully completed college and settled down with his own family. Knowing they were a great team together, they searched for new ways to work and serve together. Just about the time their son began having children of his own, they were packing their bags to be missionaries in Eastern Europe. A good team, they knew, shouldn't be wasted.

Enjoy the Experience

Talk to each other. Raising children can be difficult, energy-draining work. But it is also enjoyable work that can bring you many smiles and warm moments. Take time to enjoy those moments with each other. Remember your child will only be two years old once—enjoy it. She'll only be sweet sixteen once—enjoy it. The common memories you enjoy together will last you a lifetime.

Share Activities Together

There are many things you can do as a family that will draw you together. Find activities to do with your children that you can do together: coach a child's softball team together; memorize Bible verses together; take vacations together; serve at the church together; paint the child's room or do another family project.

CHILDREN CAN BE A WEDGE

Children should be a bond, but they can also be a wedge that drives a couple apart. This easily happens if a couple don't work together in child raising. Since working together takes effort, allowing children to become a wedge is easier than you might think.

The Load Isn't Shared

If only one spouse fills the role of parent and the other fills the role of "breadwinner," you might be headed for trouble. Even if one parent has the majority of the day-to-day parenting responsibilities, work together to set goals and solve problems. If you learn to function independently—that's his job and this is her job—you may find yourselves growing very independent of each other.

Decisions Aren't Made Together

Some of the biggest decisions will be centered on money. What should you spend money on? What's absolutely necessary and what's only a "nice-to-have"? Should you buy the sandbox, the swing set, or the new spikes for Little League? Should you buy the minivan or the Honda Accord? Resentment over how money is spent is one of the most common problems marriage counselors face. Money and other issues leave you a lot of room for discussion. If you talk and understand each other, these issues can pull you together. But there's also a lot of room for disagreement. If you leave issues and disagreements unresolved, these same things can drive you further and further apart. Rather than living with your spouse, you might as well be living with a nanny.

Discipline Problems Arise

It's critical for both parents to be of one mind when it comes to discipline. What punishments will you use for your children? When will they be enforced? If you don't agree, it won't take your child long to figure out who's the good cop and who's the bad cop. The child will get his or her way most of the time, and the parents will grow more and more frustrated with each other.

A BOND OR A WEDGE?

Children can be both. As a parent, you have the difficult endeavor to turn the challenges of parenthood into a team-building experience. Work *together*. It's a difficult task but the results are great for you *and* your children.

VALUES WORKSHEET

What is most important to you as parents? Each of you should fill out the following worksheet regarding your children, then compare and discuss your results. Rate each value 1–10 with 1 being the most important to you and 10 being the least important.

_____Know and love God
_____Work hard
_____Become a good student
_____Be socially well adapted
_____Learn to be a good friend to others
_____Develop emotionally
_____Grow up to be a good spouse and parent
_____Develop physical coordination and skills
_____Develop logical and abstract thinking
_____Develop ability to make value-driven decisions

6

GROWING TOGETHER SPIRITUALLY

How Do You Grow Together?

Couple A, married for forty years, have a phenomenal relationship. They're crazy about each other! They are viewed by many younger couples as a kind of "ideal." They are sought out by others for their wisdom and godly counsel. They're leaders in their church.

Couple B, also married for forty years, have a superficial, "Archie and Edith Bunker"-type relationship. They communicate, if at all, in small talk. They eat their meals in front of the TV set. Spiritually speaking, about the best you can say of them is "they go to church."

What's the difference? Why do so few couples keep growing together and end up being so spiritually "attractive" while most are, at best, unspectacular and, at worst, painful to look at? Four factors contribute to much marital distance and spiritual dysfunction in marriage:

1. *A misunderstanding of what marriage is*

   For many, marriage is seen as a convenient arrangement in which two individuals occupy the same house and share the same bed while living out their separate lives. In algebraic terms, this would be 1 + 1 = 2. In the biblical view, however, marriage is meant to be the dissolution of two single lives and the creation of a brand-new entity. God's marital math is 1 + 1 = 1. A husband and wife become "one flesh," which means not just physical intimacy, but a merging of lives and dreams, moving together even as they move toward God.

2. *A failure to chart a clear course*

   With no long-term vision and no agreed-upon spiritual goals or direction, marriages tend to drift. The circumstances of life, like the waves of the sea, end up propelling aimless couples to places they'd rather not go. Imagine a crew on a sailing vessel embarking on a voyage without a definite destination, and you begin to get the picture.

3. *Busyness*

Our days quickly fill up with activity. Meetings, projects, appointments—each one tied to the clock and marked "Urgent!" Unless spiritual growth and health are a top priority, a couple can be consumed quickly by the secular demands of life.

4. *Complacency*

We establish routines (or ruts). We take each other (and God) for granted. We get sluggish and lazy. Before long we are merely going through the motions. How easy it is to settle for spiritual mediocrity! How hard it is to continue following hard after God!

DO IT TOGETHER

The key component in the notion of "growing together spiritually" is the idea of "together." This implies that spiritual health must involve both parties. Husband and wife must each be growing individually before the couple can ever grow together. A weak or spiritually reluctant partner will likely drag his/her spouse down. In the same way that your spouse will be affected if you "let yourself go" physically, if you let yourself go spiritually, your spouse will suffer. You will not be able to encourage and stimulate him/her to godliness.

What concrete things can we do to ensure that we keep growing together spiritually?

Ponder and discuss together God's intent for marriage (see "What the Bible Says about Marriage on page 21"). Agree on some spiritual goals together. Pray together. Read the Bible together. Worship together. Discuss spiritual questions and insights together. Serve in the church together. Be in a small group together. Go on church retreats together.

EVERY DAY

"When my wife and I wed, someone challenged us to read God's Word and pray together daily. For the first three years of our marriage (until a rough pregnancy and the early years of parenthood!) we did that, annually reading the Bible cover to cover, using the devotional guide *The Daily Walk* (published by Walk Thru the Bible Ministries).

"Nothing before or since has meant so much to us. That morning discipline helped us lay solid spiritual foundation for our life and ministry together. We have enjoyed a long-term intimacy and unity in our relationship that I can only attribute to this practice."

—A pastor in Lousiana

How to Keep God First

THE PHENOMENON OF SPIRITUAL DRIFTING

Imagine being on a second honeymoon in Florida. You're on a raft in the warm, shallow waters of the Gulf of Mexico. Your spouse is reading a novel in a lounge chair a Frisbee throw away. You doze off and wake up minutes later to discover you're now several hundred yards down the beach. What happened? Simple. You drifted. You never intended to. But it happened nonetheless. It happened because you weren't anchored to anything. You weren't careful. Most of all, it happened because you didn't fight the pull of the waves and undertow. Now you're in a place you never wanted to go.

Putting God first or being vibrant spiritually doesn't just happen. A growing, healthy relationship with Christ must be intentionally pursued.

PULLING AT US

The phenomenon of "drifting" is constantly at work in our spiritual lives. External forces (the world, our enemy the devil) are ever pulling at us, attempting to distract us and subtly create distance in our relationship with God.

As the old hymn puts it, "Prone to wander, Lord, I feel it. Prone to leave the God I love."

Since our natural human tendency is to drift away from God, we have to be cognizant of this danger, and we have to fight it all the days of our lives.

Several facts to understand and/or remember:

- *Before God can be first in a marriage, He must be first in each of the partners' individual lives.*
  Husband, wife—first examine your own heart. Get right with God separately. Then come together and recommit your marriage to Him.
- *Growth is by grace.*
  There are no buttons on our hearts or souls that we can push to suddenly *feel excited* about God. We need help from above. If God is not first in your life, and frankly, you don't *feel* motivated to make Him first, why not be honest and admit that to God? Pray: "Lord, I need You to change my desires and to give me a deep hunger for You. If You don't transform me supernaturally, I'll never love You as I should." God loves to answer a prayer like this!

- *Putting God first requires that we do our part.*

We cannot sit around waiting for God to "zap" us. We must do what we can to put ourselves in situations where God can speak to us and change us. Get in the Word. Attend church. Listen to the sermons. Spend time praying each morning. Surround yourself with Christians (older mentor types, other couples your age) who are excited about putting God first in their lives. Let them rub off on you externally, while God works internally.

- *Whatever we are passionate about will become our priority.*

No one has to encourage a golf fanatic to "put golf first" in his or her life. Why? Because that individual has a love or passion for golf. Consequently, it's natural for him or her to want to play golf. This is true in the spiritual realm, too. If we are passionately in love with Christ, we *will* put Him first. No one will need to prod us. We don't have to tell ourselves to make our passions priorities.

WHO'S ON FIRST?

Jesus rebuked the church at Ephesus, because even though these ancient Christians maintained a moral and religious facade, their love for Christ had grown cold (see Revelation 2:1–4). Here's a checklist to help you determine whether you're keeping God first in your own life or marriage:

- Little desire to read or study God's Word
- A failure to have devotional times with God
- Infrequent communication with God throughout the day
- An indifference to spiritual matters
- A preoccupation with temporal affairs
- Spotty attendance at church
- Tension in our marriage that we are not addressing
- Complacency about the spiritual state of our neighbors and friends
- Inconsistency in areas of personal integrity and morality
- Indulgence in secret sins

Submission to Each Other and to Christ

Ephesians 5:22 is the infamous passage that instructs wives to submit to their husbands. Lifted out of its context, this verse has been used by chauvinistic Christian males through the ages to justify all kinds of marital abuse. The tragic result is that the noble concept of "submission" has become contemptible. It is anathema to most moderns (and even many believers). Any mention of the *S* word is likely to meet with a response along these lines:

> "*Willingly* give up my rights? *Voluntarily* yield to the wishes
> of another? Yeah, right! I'd just as soon commit hari-kari.
> I'm not letting anyone take advantage of me."

The problem, as noted above, is that this single command has been lifted out of its context.

How many husbands bother to read the prior verse, "Submit to one another out of reverence for Christ" (Ephesians 5:21)?

How many males ponder and meditate on the mind-boggling command that shows up just four verses later, "Husbands, love your wives, just as Christ loved the church and gave himself up for her"?

It's only as we read the whole passage and consider the overall message that we get a glimpse of what God has in mind for husbands and wives.

God's plan is for an intimate relationship that is marked by humility and kindness and others-centeredness. In a God-honoring marriage, each spouse is looking out for the best interests of the other (see Philippians 2:4). Each spouse gives up his or her own agenda, lays down his or her "rights," and seeks first and foremost to bless the other. The goal becomes to please and serve.

Loving one's wife as Christ loved the church can never mean being selfish or harsh. Christ's love commitment for and to His bride, the church, is, at the very least, unconditional, unceasing, sacrificial (not sentimental), pure, and bold.

When did Christ ever act sullen or petty? When did He ever demand

His rights? When did He ever "look out for number one"? Answer: Never. He has always sought what was best for His people. And we should do no less in our marriages.

Do you see how this kind of love makes submission not a dangerous or foolish response, but a wise course of action? If you know that your spouse is seeking your best, and if you are pursuing the same goal, suddenly there is a safety and security in the relationship that breeds trust.

And in a world of suspicion and mistrust, in an era that prizes personal autonomy and worships at the altar of individualism, in a generation where husbands and wives butt heads over every little issue, Christians have the opportunity to shock society by the simple act of submitting first to Christ and then to one another.

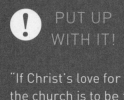

PUT UP WITH IT!

"If Christ's love for the church is to be the model for marriage, then this much both partners can learn: you have to put up with a lot, and you have to cherish a lot."
—George McCauley

Choosing a Church

A popular myth embraced by many in our culture (including many self-proclaimed believers in Christ) is that spirituality is a private thing, a personal matter. Church is seen as irrelevant and unnecessary. "I don't need to go to church. I can worship God all by myself."

Forgotten is the clear command of God:
"And let us consider how we may spur one another on toward love and good deeds, not giving up meeting together, as some are in the habit of doing, but encouraging one another—and all the more as you see the Day approaching" (Hebrews 10:24–25).

BURNING COALS

"The virtuous soul that is alone. . .is like the burning coal that is alone. It will grow colder rather than hotter."
—John of the Cross

Perhaps this antichurch trend stems from our American love of individualism or our aversion to commitment, but one thing is clear: it *doesn't* come from the Bible! In scripture, faith is always (and only) lived out in the context of community. God has designed us so that we need one another and so that we are healthy only when we live interdependently. For this reason Christians are never portrayed as independent, isolated entities in the Bible, but as "parts" of the larger body of Christ (1 Corinthians 12), as "members" of God's household or family, and as building blocks in God's temple (Ephesians 2).

Practically speaking, the New Testament pattern is that Christians need to belong to a local church body. This is *not* optional, though many modern-day believers live as though it were. It is only in this context that we live out our divine calling: maturing in Christ (or growing) and ministering for Him (serving).

Since church is intended by God to be *the* crucial component in our spiritual journey, it's important to find a good one.

Here are the marks of a New Testament church:

1. A Passion for God

Look for a body of believers that embraces the scriptural truth that we were created "by God and for God." Such a church will be consumed with the greatness of God. They will be marked by a "He is the point!" spirit. Such hunger and passion for God will be demonstrated by powerful worship, lavish giving, and glad serving.

2. A Preoccupation with Prayer

Healthy churches and significant works of God have one thing in common. They are steeped in prayer. Prayer is not secondary. It is not viewed as an "extra" or "tacked-on" activity. It is primary. Look for a praying church, marked by unceasing corporate dependence on God.

WHY BOTHER?

"We should leave a worship service asking ourselves not 'What did I get out of it?' but rather 'Was God pleased with what happened?'"
—Philip Yancey, *Church: Why Bother?*

3. The Presence of True Community

Try to find a body of people that enjoys authentic fellowship in the midst of an artificial age. The early Church "shared life together" (the definition of biblical fellowship), not just attended meetings with one another.

4. The Priority of Local Witness

Look for a congregation whose members actively pursue redemptive relationships with their lost neighbors, friends, and colleagues. Members "show" Christ by their actions, but they also "tell" others about Him as a way of life. A witnessing church is a healthy church.

5. The Priority of Global Outreach

A New Testament church understands that, since God has the whole world on His heart, they, too, need to embrace a comprehensive perspective on outreach. They make the effort to be *informed* of God's global activity and seek to become more *involved* in praying, giving, and going—"to the ends of the earth"!

6. A Practice of Equipping Believers

Jesus' call to make disciples begins at home. A church can't reach its neighbors, much less the world, unless it is seeking to build mature, trained witnesses. Seek to find a church that teaches God's Word and that is permeated by an equipping mentality—one that builds up its members so that they can do "the work of ministry" (Ephesians 4:12 NKJV).

7. The Proliferation of Lay Servants/Ministers

In most churches, the 20–80 rule applies (20 percent of the members do 80 percent of the serving and giving). This is an indictment of Western Christianity's consumer mentality. A human body in which certain organs/parts do nothing or fulfill their function only occasionally is said to be paralyzed, handicapped, or sick. The same is true in Christ's body, the Church, when members opt not to participate. A healthy church pushes its members to use their gifts to build up the body.

HERE'S A THOUGHT

"As I look around on Sunday morning at the people populating the pews, I see the risk that God has assumed. For whatever reason, God now reveals himself in the world not through a pillar of smoke and fire, not even through the physical body of his Son in Galilee, but through the mongrel collection that comprises my local church and every other such gathering in God's name."
—Philip Yancey, *Church: Why Bother?*

When you find a good church (Note: You'll never find a perfect one!), here's what to do to make the experience great:

- Attend (rather than sleep in)
- Join (rather than remain uncommitted)
- Listen (rather than snooze)
- Volunteer (rather than sit back)
- Serve (rather than consume)
- Give (rather than hoard)
- Pray (rather than criticize)
- Submit to the leaders (rather than oppose)
- Invite (rather than be self-centered)

Ministry Opportunities

Marriage is the merging of two lives, not merely for the establishment of a new household, but for the creation of a new entity *that is able to have an eternal impact.*

It's easy in our narcissistic age to forget that marriage was never intended by God to be an orgy of self-preoccupation. Acquiring lovely possessions, creating a *House Beautiful* look—these are worthless if we don't use our homes and marriages for heaven's sake. God wants the couples who claim to love Him to serve Him. He designed marriage to fulfill a divine mission. In short, He wants us to team up with our spouses for the goal of ministering to a lost and needy world.

More Christian couples need to follow the biblical example of Priscilla and Aquila. What a TEAM! In Acts 18, we note. . .

- They were well versed in God's **T**ruth (and thus able to help teach younger believers the ways of God). *How well do you know the scriptures?*
- They kept an eye on **E**ternity (that is, they were more concerned about the spiritual and eternal needs of others than they were material and temporal things like career, houses, possessions, etc.). *Are you more concerned with laying up treasure on earth or with investing in eternity?*
- They had an attitude of **A**vailability (moving as needed at the apostle Paul's request from Corinth to Ephesus to Rome then back to Ephesus to do the work of God—see 1 Corinthians 16:19; Romans 16:3–5; 2 Timothy 4:19). *Are you willing to go and do and be whatever God asks? Do you make your possessions available for kingdom purpose?*
- They were radically committed to **M**inistry (touching lives everywhere they went, when it was convenient and when it wasn't). *Are you intertwined in the lives of people—seeking to spur them on to a deeper relationship with God?*

HEADS UP!

"Let temporal things serve your use, but the eternal be the object of your desire."
—Thomas à Kempis

THE POWER OF HOSPITALITY

Romans 12:13 commands believers in Jesus to "practice hospitality." Hospitality is that act of welcoming others into our homes where they can be loved, accepted, fed, served, and ministered to. The result is that they leave replenished and with full stomachs, if not hearts. Karen Mains has written these challenging words in her book *Open Heart, Open Home*:

"Many of us have been given a most remarkable tool through which to minister—the miracle of a Christian home. I am firmly convinced that if Christians would open their homes and practice hospitality as defined in scripture, we could significantly alter the fabric of society. We could play a major role in its spiritual, moral, and emotional redemption."

Ministry Ideas for Couples:
- Volunteer to teach a Sunday school class at church.
- Get involved in neighborhood functions—block parties, neighborhood watches, etc.
- Serve on school committees, parent-teacher councils, etc.
- Agree to coach Little League sports.
- Host a Bible study or small group in your home.
- Bring a cake/pie/cookies to the new neighbors.
- Do the Cub Scout/Brownie/Boy Scout/Girl Scout thing.
- Watch a young couple's children so they can have a night out.
- Befriend the international family that lives on your street.
- Make your home a kid magnet—the place where others are drawn. Invest in things like a basketball hoop, a pool table, a Ping-Pong table.
- Work at creating a comfy, cozy feel in your living room—make it an oasis where others are drawn.

- Commit your home, your minivan, your ski boat, your camp, etc. to the work of Christ. Offer it up for His use.
- If you live near a university, invite a collegiate or two home for Sunday lunch.
- Use your natural gifts and abilities to serve others. Bake for the kingdom. Do yard work for Christ's sake.

Encouragement from the Bible

Consider how living out these "one anothers" and "each others" could (and would!) transform your marriage relationship (emphasis added):

John 13:34	"A new command I give you: *Love one another.*"
Romans 12:10	"*Be devoted to one another* in love."
Romans 12:10	"*Honor one another* above yourselves."
Romans 12:16	"*Live in harmony with one another.*"
Romans 14:13	"Therefore let us *stop passing judgment on one another.*"
Romans 15:7	"*Accept one another*, then, just as Christ accepted you."
1 Corinthians 7:5	"*Do not deprive each other* [sexually] except perhaps by mutual consent and for a time."
Galatians 5:13	"*Serve one another* humbly in love."
Galatians 5:26	"Let us not become conceited, *provoking and envying each other.*"
Ephesians 4:2	"Be patient, *bearing with one another* in love."
Ephesians 4:32	"*Be kind and compassionate to one another.*"
Ephesians 5:19	"*Speaking to one another with psalms, hymns and songs from the Spirit.*"
Ephesians 5:21	"*Submit to one another* out of reverence for Christ."
Colossians 3:9	"*Do not lie to each other.*"

Colossians 3:13	*"Forgive one another."*
Colossians 3:16	*"Admonish one another* with all wisdom."
1 Thessalonians 3:12	*"May the Lord make your love increase and overflow for each other."*
1 Thessalonians 5:11	"Therefore *encourage one another* and *build each other up."*
1 Thessalonians 5:15	"Make sure that nobody pays back wrong for wrong, but always *strive to do what is good for each other."*
Hebrews 10:24	"Let us consider how we may *spur one another on toward love and good deeds."*
James 4:11	"Brothers and sisters, *do not slander one another."*
James 5:9	*"Don't grumble against one another."*
James 5:16	"Therefore *confess your sins to each other* and *pray for each other* so that you may be healed."
1 Peter 4:9	*"Offer hospitality to one another."*
1 Peter 5:5	"All of you, *clothe yourselves with humility toward one another."*

Remember, these are not optional suggestions but rather mandatory commands.

Remember, too, that God has given us everything we need to live as He expects (2 Peter 1:3). These behaviors are impossible if we live in our own strength; they become realities when we walk in the power of the Spirit (Galatians 5:16).

A "Mission Statement" for Your Marriage

In his bestselling book, *The Seven Habits of Highly Effective People,* author Stephen Covey advocates the practice of writing a "personal mission statement." Such a unique document "focuses on what you want to be (character) and to do (contributions and achievements) and on the values or principles upon which being and doing are based."

Many individuals have found that such a written creed has helped them stay focused on what matters most in life. Acting as a kind of "personal constitution," a mission statement serves as a helpful guide for daily decision making. It keeps us on track spiritually, morally, and relationally so that when we get to the end of life we do not look back and feel large measures of regret.

Married couples can also benefit greatly from this process of careful planning and intentional living.

Here are some ways you can stop reacting to life and start living proactively in your marriage:

1. *Take a long, hard look at your own character.* Assess your strengths and weaknesses. Take stock of your gifts and abilities, as well as the blessings and experiences God has put in your life. Think back over your successes and failures. Analyze your God-given passions (e.g., a desire to make a difference in a certain area).

   What do you need to change about yourself? Where do you need divine help? What qualities are you proud of? What habits do you need to eliminate?

   This can be a very uncomfortable, even painful exercise. But by honest assessment, you can begin minimizing your weaknesses and maximizing your strengths. Also (as AA has discovered), it's only when we admit we have problems in certain areas that we begin to humbly seek help.

2. *Envision yourselves at the end of life.* It's your sixtieth or sixty-fifth wedding anniversary, say, and you're gathered with your children and grandchildren (maybe even great-grandchildren!). They are throwing a big surprise shindig for you and reflecting on your life together. They are telling stories and expressing their love.

   What memories do you want them to have? What accomplishments do you want to be able to look back over—relationships (with God and with others), impact on the world for eternity's sake, service to others, career achievements, etc.? What character qualities do you want them to remember about you? What values do you want your children and their descendants to have caught and to be in the process of passing on? In short, what kind of legacy do you want to leave?

3. *Talk to your spouse at length about your values, hopes, dreams, and ideals.* (This may even be the subject of a weekend away together.) This is deeper than "One day I hope we can buy a ski boat and a camp on a lake in the country." This is more along the lines of "I want us to be a family that is radically committed to Jesus Christ in every way!" or "My dream is that it could truly be said of us that we poured out our lives in love for and service to God and people."

   Think specifically about these matters. Plan on spending a long time on this exercise. Don't imagine you can complete this assignment while you're watching *Wheel of Fortune!* In essence, you are trying to summarize all that you want to live for into a concise statement. You are writing your epitaph in advance.

4. *Prayerfully begin backing up.* Envision what you need to do now to get to where you'd like to end up. This is where goals come into play. You need long-term goals to point you in the right overall direction, and you need short-term goals to keep you on track day by day and week by week.

Marital goal setting (after you've established an overall mission statement).

What specific things do you want to accomplish. . .

Spiritually (relationship with God)?
In your family (relating to parents, children, etc.)?
Physically (maintaining your health and fitness)?
In ministry (church involvement and serving others)?
Financially (giving, saving, and spending money)?

Socially (maintaining and developing friendships)?
Vocationally (career and/or employment situations)?
Recreationally (leisure activities, vacations, etc.)?
Intellectually (continued mental growth and stimulation)?

Interfaith Marriages

Both the biblical record and contemporary experience demonstrate the difficulty of interfaith marriages.

King Solomon married foreign wives (who had very different religious beliefs), and it cost him greatly (see 1 Kings 11). Some would blame all his marital troubles on the different cultural backgrounds of his wives or on his sinful polygamy, but it's hard to deny that much of his domestic difficulty and internal turmoil (see Ecclesiastes) was due to the simple fact that he was intimately involved with those who did not share his spiritual convictions.

Even the New Testament (see 2 Corinthians 6) warns about entering close relationships with those of a different faith (or those of no faith).

The best advice (since marriage is hard enough even when you share similar beliefs) is to marry someone whose faith closely mirrors your own.

The problems become even more pronounced when sweethearts who embrace totally different religious systems attempt to marry. For example, a Buddhist and a Baptist (if they were serious adherents to their faith) or a Mormon and a Jew would find little upon which to agree.

Every situation is different, every couple is unique, but the short answer to the interfaith marriage question is generally "Don't!" At the spiritual level (which is the foundational level of any good marriage), you want to be on the same page with your spouse. If you are constantly bickering about (or just as bad, if you cannot even discuss) your most cherished beliefs about God, eternity, etc., you will miss out on the greatest joy of marriage.

If you do decide to enter into an interfaith relationship (or find yourself already in one), be forewarned. You will need to. . .

Work at learning about the differences. Visit the library. Study up. Get the facts.

Work at accepting the differences. Don't make the mistake of assuming that you can change your spouse, that he or she will eventually see things your way. Such an expectation (or demanding spirit) paves the way for serious marital discord.

Work at talking through the differences. Though your natural tendency will likely be to avoid bringing up this constantly contentious issue, you need to learn to discuss it without emotional fireworks.

Work at developing a clear, well-communicated plan for how your differing beliefs will be lived out—especially with regard to the children. Almost no other area generates as much friction. Many

 WHICH CHURCH?

The degree of difficulty in an interfaith marriage is directly dependent on the degree of difference in the faiths. An Episcopalian and a Catholic will generally not have as much disagreement or trouble as a Baptist and a Catholic. Even though these are all "Christian" denominations, there are doctrinal differences between them, sometimes major.

children end up turned off to religion altogether because of the way their parents tried to use them as pawns in their ongoing religious squabbles.

The key word? *Work.* It takes a lot of work to make an interfaith marriage work. This is no place for the lazy or squeamish.

 EYES OPEN OR CLOSED?

"Go into marriage with both eyes wide open. After you say 'I do' keep eyes half shut."

—Benjamin Franklin

Good Devotional Books for Couples

Which of the following would make the biggest spiritual impact on your marriage?

(a) Weekly marital counseling with Gary Smalley and James Dobson
(b) A month-long trip to the Holy Land with Chuck Swindoll
(c) Memorizing the New Testament together
(d) Having Reverend and Mrs. Billy Graham move in with you to mentor you and your spouse for a whole year
(e) All of the above

The answer is probably "All of the above." However, the odds of those things happening in your life are about the same as the odds of Hades dipping permanently below the 32-degree mark.

So what CAN you do. . .realistically?

You and your spouse can do daily devotions together. Call it a quiet time, family altar, the morning watch, whatever. The fact is, couples who read God's Word and pray together daily generally are healthier and happier than those who don't.

Your Christian bookstore probably has dozens of different devotional books and guides (and new ones are being published all the time). However, you may wish to try one of the following titles:

- *God Calling*. A bestselling devotional guide published by Barbour and read by millions daily.
- *The Daily Walk*. This popular devotional magazine takes you through the whole Bible in a year and is published by Walk Thru the Bible Ministries of Atlanta, Georgia.
- *Life Lessons from Bible People*. This creative Tyndale publication offers 366 short devotions from the lives of both prominent and little-known Bible characters.
- *Life Application Family Devotions*. Part of the bestselling Life Application® line of Bibles and Bible study materials, this highly practical devotional guide from Tyndale House offers a topical approach to the everyday issues couples and families face.
- *My Utmost for His Highest* by Oswald Chambers. Perhaps the granddaddy of all devotional books. Rich, meaty, powerful!
- *God's Little Devotional Book for Couples* by Honor Books, one of the leading publishers of devotional materials.
- *Becoming Soul Mates* by marital "experts" Les and Leslie Parrott and published by Zondervan contains fifty-two devotions for new couples.
- *Devotions for Couples* (Zondervan) by bestselling author Patrick Morley is subtitled "For Busy Couples Who Want More Intimacy in Their Relationships."
- *Moments with the Savior* is a profoundly touching devotional book by Ken Gire, one of Christianity's premier writers. It's published by Zondervan.

PRAY TOGETHER!

"Couples who frequently pray together are twice as likely as those who pray less often to describe their marriages as being highly romantic. And get this—married couples who pray together are 90 percent more likely to report higher satisfaction with their sex lives than couples who don't pray together. Prayer, because of the vulnerability it demands, also draws a couple closer."
—Les and Leslie Parrott, *Marriage Partnership* magazine

7

HUSBANDS AND WIVES

Differences between Men and Women

A REAL DIFFERENCE

Besides the obvious anatomical differences, and the fact that NASA researchers now believe males are from the planet Mars and females originated on Venus (a fact all but confirmed by several bestselling nonfiction books), the sexes are quite unique.

Consider that these are broad generalizations with a large number of exceptions, but still accurate in many instances:

Men tend to be...	Women tend to be...
More physical	More verbal
Physically stronger	Physically weaker
Compartmentalized in their thinking	"Global"/holistic in their thinking
Oblivious to feelings	More in touch with feelings
Goal-oriented	People-/need-oriented
Logical thinkers	Intuitive thinkers
Eager to achieve	Eager to belong
More assured	More in need of assurance
Dependent on work and family for significance	Dependent on husband for significance
Wired to watch forty-seven programs at a time	Wired to watch one channel at a time
Too proud to ask for help	Too smart NOT to ask for help
Into movies like *Dumb and Dumber*	Into movies like *Jane Eyre* and *Howard's End*
More aware of the models in the *Sports Illustrated* swimsuit issue	More drawn to the actual *swimsuits*
Sexually aroused by sight	Sexually aroused by touch

DEALING WITH THE DIFFERENCES

Okay, all this talk about the sexes. Now what? Well, we have several options. We can. . .

(a.) **Deny** the differences. This makes about as much sense as denying the law of gravity. Men and women are fundamentally different, and all the social engineering in the world can't alter this truth! Neither sex is better; each is distinct and unique.

WISDOM FOR WOMEN

"It's a well-known fact that a male with even a moderate testosterone level would rather drill a hole in his hand (which he probably will) than admit, especially to his spouse, that he cannot do something himself."

—Dave Barry

"It's a good thing there's not a third sex, or women would be in big trouble."

—An unmarried forty-year-old guy

(b.) **Ignore** the differences. Why not take advantage of life-enhancing, relationship-enriching information?

(c.) **Seek to understand** the differences. A wise man or woman will make his or her sweetheart/ spouse a subject of long-term, intense scrutiny. You will never figure him/her out. The human soul has depths no one but God knows. But you can, with effort, learn to move on to the next phase.

(d.) **Accept** the differences. Imagine how dull the world would be if we didn't have the opposite sex around to shake our heads at. Sure, they're weird, but in a fascinating kind of way.

(e.) **Celebrate** the differences. Don't just tolerate the opposite sex! Celebrate God's genius! In perfect wisdom He made it so that when Adam and Eve came together like a two-piece jigsaw puzzle, they formed a new entity, something whole and complete. (And note that He pronounced it "very good"!) Nothing has changed through the ages.

There's still a wonderfully satisfying fit when a husband and wife bring their wildly different personalities, perspectives, attitudes, and bodies together and connect spiritually, emotionally, and physically. It's a miracle that such diverse creatures could ever be called "one." But that's precisely what God does!

WISDOM FOR MEN

Young son: "Is what I heard true, Dad, that in some parts of Africa a man doesn't know his wife until he marries her?"
Dad: "That happens in every country, son."

His Needs, Her Needs

Because men and women are wired differently, their needs are different, too. It's important that both parties understand and talk about each other's needs to avoid lasting conflict. Unmet needs are very frustrating and lead to an unfulfilling marriage.

There's a good, popular Christian book that's worth reading: *His Needs, Her Needs* by Willard F. Harley Jr. (published by Revell). Dr. Harley gives what he considers the top five marital needs for men and the top five marital needs for women. Their lists, as you'd expect, are very different. We'll summarize his opinion on the next few pages.

On the next page are ten basic marital needs. Which five do you think are the husband's needs? Which is the most important to him? Which five for the wife? Which is the most important to her? Rank the top five for the husband and the top five for the wife before you continue reading.

Ten Basic Relationship Needs	Wife's Top Five Needs	Husband's Top Five Needs
Admiration		
Affection		
An attractive spouse		
Conversation		
Domestic support		
Family commitment		
Financial support		
Honesty and openness		
Recreational companionship		
Sexual fulfillment		

HER FIRST NEED: AFFECTION

To a woman, affection symbolizes security, comfort, and approval. Know that your wife's need for affection stems from her desire to be loved and cared for. Sex and affection should come hand in hand. Affection allows your wife to feel cherished and meaningful. A little effort in the area of a hug or kiss goes a long way in boosting a woman's confidence in her husband's love for her.

HIS FIRST NEED: SEXUAL FULFILLMENT

While women have a deep need for affection, men have a deep need to be fulfilled sexually. Your husband hopes for you to be willingly available when he has a desire to make love. A man trusts his wife to be as sexually interested in him as he is in her. It is important for you, as a couple, to find sexual compatibility by communicating your sexual expectations.

SHE NEEDS: CONVERSATION

Verbal attention is a great way to let wives know that they are cared for. It allows them to express desires and concerns and also shows them that continuing to get to know them is important. Conversation on a daily basis sometimes takes effort because it takes time away from other things. But take that time and ask her about her day, the people she may have encountered, and most importantly, her feelings about the events that occurred. By giving your wife individual attention through conversation, she will feel loved and valued.

HE NEEDS: RECREATIONAL COMPANIONSHIP

A man places a surprising amount of value on spending time with his wife while doing things that he enjoys. The person you are with while experiencing the most enjoyable moments of your life is the person you will feel closely bonded with. A woman who seeks to have a fulfilling marriage should join her husband in these recreational activities. So find hobbies that you *both* enjoy and enjoy them *together*.

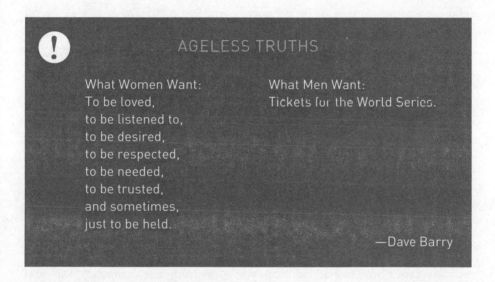

! AGELESS TRUTHS

What Women Want:
To be loved,
to be listened to,
to be desired,
to be respected,
to be needed,
to be trusted,
and sometimes,
just to be held.

What Men Want:
Tickets for the World Series.

—Dave Barry

SHE NEEDS: HONESTY AND OPENNESS

A woman's trust in her husband provides security and stability in the relationship. Be honest with your wife so that she trusts you to give her the information that she needs. If you present yourself as you are, it allows your wife to adapt, adjust, and grow closer to you. Men who do not keep open and honest communication with their wives eventually break down their wives' confidence and cause them to lose security in the relationship. So be truthful so your wife can better know how to love you.

HE NEEDS: AN ATTRACTIVE SPOUSE

Being attractive to your husband goes a long way in letting him know that you care about his happiness. You don't have to look like a beauty queen, but desiring to please him by your appearance should be something you strive for. Try something small like fixing your hair in a different way or putting on a nice outfit. You might be surprised at your husband's reaction to your improved look.

SHE NEEDS: FINANCIAL SUPPORT

Having enough money to be supported and live comfortably is a powerful need that women often feel. If your wife works, give her the option of staying home while you support her and the family. Ask her if she feels satisfied with the amount of money you make. No matter what your income, every family must recognize what they can afford. Make a budget and use it as a stepping-stone to reach the financial goals you're both comfortable with.

HE NEEDS: DOMESTIC SUPPORT

On a smaller degree, men also have a desire to be taken care of. This comes more in the context of having a maintained house with well-behaved kids and a pleasant greeting at the door after work. If your husband comes home to a house in shambles, it does nothing to ease the stress from his workday. Since, both husband and wife work in many marriages, it's important to find out what your husband desires from you concerning the domestic duties and to convey how you expect him to be instrumental in them as well. Create a plan to help in developing household roles that promote mutual support.

SHE NEEDS: FAMILY COMMITMENT

Your wife needs you to be a good father. Having a strong family unit is something that provides emotional security and contentment for her. Most wives desire their husbands to take a leadership role in the family and with the children. In making an effort to contribute to the moral and educational development of your children, you will show your wife that you are willing to make the effort to benefit the family as a whole. Recognizing that parenting takes training is the first step to being committed to the family. Learning how to be consistent, punishing properly, and reaching agreements with your wife are all things that you can do to show her that your desire is to be a good father.

HE NEEDS: ADMIRATION

Your husband needs you to be proud of him. When a woman compliments her husband, it inspires him to achieve more. It gives him the motivation to take on new responsibilities and reach for higher goals. Let your husband know what you admire in him for what he is today and not for what he has the ability to achieve in the future. Criticism often leads to pessimism, but encouragement leads to greater potential. Boost your husband's self-esteem by letting him know exactly what you appreciate about him.

IN CONCLUSION

Each of these summaries is explored further in Dr. Harley's book, and it should be read for further discussion.

While these might be good guidelines, each couple will be different. The most important trait to you might not even be listed here. What your top five needs are isn't as important as *talking* about them. Men and women are different. Your needs differ. Talk about what you feel and what you need. Your marriage will be better.

8

SEX, MONEY, AND OTHER ISSUES

A Healthy Sexual Relationship

Here it is, the chapter you've been waiting for. . . . Forget all that other stuff about communication, dividing chores, praying together, etc. Let's get to the point. Let's talk about SEX! Yowsa! Get out the oysters and other aphrodisiacs. Light some candles. Slip into something more comfortable, baby! This is what marriage is really all about, right?

Wrong. Sex is an important part (and a very fun part!) of marriage, but it's not the most important aspect. Not by a long shot.

WHY DID GOD CREATE SEX?

The Bible seems to give two broad reasons or purposes for sex. At an obvious, biological level, sex was designed by God for the propagation of the human race (Genesis 1:27–28; Psalm 127). This is the great rebuttal to the modern-day claim that homosexuality is natural and normal. Strictly practiced, homosexuality would result in the extinction of humankind! Sex was also created by God for enjoyment and pleasure (see the Song of Solomon).

SEX IS NOT SIN

"Contrary to Mrs. Grundy, sex is not sin. Contrary to Hugh Hefner, it's not salvation either. Like nitroglycerin, it can be used either to blow up bridges or heal hearts."
—Frederick Buechner, *Wishful Thinking*

Like so many other things, sex is intended to be a visible picture of invisible realities. A man and woman who are wholeheartedly devoted to each other and enjoying deep spiritual and emotional intimacy come together physically to express their love and commitment. It is a marvelously sacred thing, a mysteriously holy act intended to signify utter unity and fidelity. What a contrast to the cheap, worldly caricature of sex as "no big deal; a physical act that, if you take the necessary precautions, is devoid of any real consequences."

It follows, then, that premarital sex is a violation of God's standard. It distorts God's plan in that it results in a premature intimacy/consummation/unity (Hebrews 13:4). And extramarital sex is abhorrent and evil because it is an outright betrayal of one's pledge to remain singularly devoted to one's marital partner. Since the marriage between a husband and wife is intended to mirror Christ's relationship with His church, unfaithfulness destroys this picture of devotion (Ephesians 5; Colossians 3:5; 2 Corinthians 11:1–3).

Some signs of an unhealthy sexual relationship:
- Lots of physical involvement with little other deep emotional or spiritual interaction
- Pressure by one partner to do things the other partner is uncomfortable with
- The withholding of sex (by either party) as a weapon or as leverage in the relationship
- The use of (or demand for) sex to "atone" for other relational failures
- Any use of pornography
- Repeated mechanical, passionless, "quickie" encounters
- Indifference by either party to the other's sexual pleasure
- Extreme selfishness by either party
- Phobic fear of being seen naked by one's spouse (especially after being married for a while)
- So-called rough sex
- Anything that is intentionally physically painful to one or both parties (e.g., sadomasochistic behavior) (Note: Those experiencing *unintentional* pain during intercourse—or any other sexual dysfunction—should consult a medical expert.)
- Ongoing reluctance or outright refusal by one or both parties to engage in sexual relations (Note: This is usually a sign of deeper problems in the relationship.)
- Reducing sex in one's mind to an issue of male and/or female genitalia reaching orgasm (so much so that one fails to enjoy the whole process and the whole person)
- Excessive masturbation by either or both parties
- A desire by one or both parties to do sexually risky things (e.g.,

have sex in public places, use video cameras, bondage, etc.)

- Fantasies that involve other people or kinky activities that would not honor God

Some good sexual reminders:

If you're engaged (or reading this on your honeymoon):

1. It is normal to feel a little scared and/or embarrassed.
2. You both may experience feelings of disappointment on your wedding night. Why? It's difficult to think of another human experience that is so eagerly anticipated and that carries with it such lofty expectations. It's almost as if we set ourselves up for certain disappointment. We've seen too many movies and read too many magazine articles. The truth is, many women (especially those who are virgins) report feelings of discomfort when having intercourse for the first time. Many sexually inexperienced men have problems with premature ejaculation.

GOOD READIN'

Every Christian married couple would greatly benefit by purchasing and reading *Intended for Pleasure* by Dr. Ed Wheat. This comprehensive guide published by Revell offers sane, God-honoring counsel for the various sexual questions that couples face. Highly recommended!

3. You don't have to know *everything*. (But you *do* need to know some basic things. If you don't already have one, purchase a good book on marital sex immediately and begin reading. See sidebar.)
4. You don't have to *do* everything. (Especially the first night or even in the first month or year! Counselors routinely visit with shell-shocked brides who were subjected to every sexual position and practice on their honeymoons by husbands who were "raring to go" and eager to try everything they'd ever heard of.)

Here are some other things to keep in mind:

- For all married couples (newlyweds, middle-agers, and golden oldies), let your physical relationship be playful and fun. It's not called forePLAY for nothing.
- It is okay to laugh—even during sex. In fact, it is probably healthy! Don't take yourself (or your sexual prowess) too seriously.
- Be spontaneous and creative. You don't have to *always* do the same thing, the same way. Leave it to us humans to take something as exciting and amazing as sex and make it dull and boring.
- Learn to discuss openly and honestly your feelings and desires with regard to marital sex. We remind you again: you did not marry a mind reader. Your spouse cannot know what you're thinking unless you open your mouth and use nouns, verbs, and adjectives. (Adverbs are a nice touch, too!)
- You don't have to meet anyone else's expectations (or compete statistically with other couples). Forget the Kinsey Report (it's been debunked anyway) and the Gallup Poll and your bigmouthed friend.
- Sex, like any other activity, becomes more enjoyable the more you know and the more experienced you become (assuming, of course, that your relationship is healthy in other areas!).
- Sex can never make a bad relationship good. What you do *out of* bed will affect the quality of what goes on *in* bed—not the other way around.
- Husbands and wives need to consider each other as more important than themselves. Being other-centered is the fastest way for two people to enjoy a healthy and satisfying sex life.
- You have a lifetime to figure it out. So relax and enjoy yourselves!

How to Ruin Your Sexual Relationship

The world is full of people—married people, married CHRISTIANS—who have dreadful sex lives. If you don't believe that, ask any marriage counselor. They daily hear the sob stories of believers who, when it comes to sex, are either frustrated or frigid, bored or burned out, wallowing in shame or burning with bitterness.

How could something that has the potential to be so wonderful and fun end up being such a miserable experience? Every couple is unique, and the details of every situation vary. But here are a few universal factors that are pretty well guaranteed to ruin your sexual relationship in marriage.

Neglect the other dimensions of married life.

Sex was designed by God to be a physical expression of a couple's spiritual and emotional intimacy. As such, it is much more than a mere physical act; it involves all that we are as people. That's why sex between two people (even married Christians) who are not connecting at the heart and soul levels feels superficial and cheap. Oh, it might be physically fulfilling (in the short term), but it can never be emotionally satisfying (in the long term). Couples who pursue physical intimacy without a corresponding spiritual and emotional intimacy will one day wake up to find that physical pleasure is not enough to hold a relationship together.

Be selfish.

Self-centeredness is at the core of most marital difficulties, and so it's not surprising to find it present when couples are struggling sexually. What does "selfish sexuality" look like? It's the husband who never considers his wife's desires, who is interested in her only until he reaches a climax. It's the wife who uses sex as a weapon or as leverage, who, with cruel intent, deprives her husband of sex. The great calling of believers is to consider others as more important than ourselves. Certainly this applies to couples and marital sex. Forgotten by many married Christians is the amazing biblical truth that our bodies actually belong to our spouses (1 Corinthians 7:3–4) and that we are not to deprive each other sexually (1 Corinthians 7:5).

DO YOUR PART

"Put to death, therefore, whatever belongs to your earthly nature: sexual immorality, impurity, lust, evil desires and greed, which is idolatry."

Colossians 3:5

Have unrealistic expectations.

Some husbands and wives live under a whole host of sexual myths, misconceptions, and fallacies. One of the most dangerous legends is that everyone else is having more sex or better sex. As soon as a spouse begins thinking this way, he or she often begins feeling disillusioned and/or disgusted. Forget the surveys and polls. Flush the anecdotes of immodest friends. You're not competing with anyone else. Trying to do so only leads to trouble.

Indulge in pornography.

Lewd videos, erotic Internet images, and sexually explicit books and magazines have done more to wreck the sex lives of married couples than almost anything else. What wife can compete with the surgically enhanced women of porn and their computer-altered images? Pornography treats women as sex objects, existing only for the purpose of gratifying men's sexual desires. Furthermore, it demeans God's wonderful gift of sexual love in marriage. Stay away from it. It is addictive and dangerous. If you think you might have a problem, call the American Family Association (1-601-844-5128) or Focus on the Family (1-800-A-FAMILY). Both of these ministries have trained counselors who can assist you in getting the help you need.

Ask your mate to do something that violates his/her conscience.
That couple in the movie who, um, engaged in, uh, some sizzling hanky-panky, um. . .you remember, the scene in the department store dressing room? Hey, that kind of stuff is Hollywood fantasy, and not something you ought to pressure your quiet, reserved spouse into doing! The point is this: your spouse may not be as "liberated" as you think you are, and if you force him or her into activities that cause feelings of weirdness, guess what? He or she will become even LESS liberated!

Be unfaithful.
Probably the single most ruinous thing you can do to your spouse (and to your relationship) is to commit adultery. Assuming he or she stays with you (and that's a big IF), there will be mistrust and disgust for a long time. God can heal these kinds of situations, but there will always be regrets and scars. Please don't succumb to this temptation.

Identifying and Overcoming Problems

"Into every life a little rain must fall," the old saying goes, and if we apply that truth to husbands and wives, it becomes "Into every marriage some problems must come." The issue really isn't "What will we do IF hard times come?" but "How will we respond WHEN trials do come?"

The following are some things couples can do to identify and solve their problems early rather than passively sitting back and waiting till their marital troubles are overwhelming:

A narrow road twisting up and through the Swiss Alps featured lots of beautiful views. . .and just as many dangerous, hairpin turns. One particular stretch of road was notorious for the large number of motorists who innocently plummeted off its narrow shoulder into the valley below. One morning, after yet another gruesome crash, concerned residents in a nearby village huddled and concluded they must do something about these frequent accidents. One man suggested building a high, heavy-duty guardrail along the cliff's edge. But townspeople objected, arguing that such a project would spoil the beautiful view. After much discussion it was agreed that the town would build and staff a medical clinic in the valley where many of the cars came to rest.

Regular, honest evaluation

It was Socrates who said, "The unexamined life is not worth living." And yet most of us seldom (if ever) take the time to stop and consider what we are doing and why. If you're married (and you must be, or you wouldn't be reading this book), it's important to spend time regularly analyzing and evaluating your marital relationship. You need to ask yourself hard questions. And you need to be willing to answer them honestly.

Regular "marital summits"

It's a good idea for couples to get away periodically to work on their marriage. Such extended dates or weekends are not primarily for the purpose of dining, seeing movies, and participating in recreational pursuits (though some of those activities can be incorporated into your time away). The real purpose of such times is to engage in in-depth conversations and long-term marital planning. The goal is to talk proactively about substantive issues and to pursue real intimacy in marriage. The widely respected "Marriage Encounter" weekends are ideal for couples who feel the need for a marriage checkup but don't know how to begin.

Reading challenging books about marriage

Every married person ought to make it a priority to read one or two good books on marriage each year. Such publications (often by noted marriage experts like Gary Smalley, Larry Crabb, Norman Wright, James Dobson) can serve to encourage, challenge, convict, and motivate you to work at strengthening your marriage. As you read along, you'll find yourself saying or thinking, "Wow! Why don't we do that in our marriage?" or "Oh man. I'm guilty of that same thing!" It's basically great marital counseling, at the cost of a book! Another idea is to subscribe to a periodical like *Marriage Partnership*, by the same people who bring you *Christianity Today*. This highly practical magazine (printed six times a year) is jam-packed with helpful marital advice and tips.

Accountability

Ideally, every married couple need another Christian couple or two to help push and prod them toward marital maturity. Ask God to help you find some married friends with whom you can be honest and real, and with whom you can develop healthy relationships of accountability. An older, wiser, "mentor-like" couple is ideal, but a couple your own age is a great gift, too. Over the years you can serve as role models for one another, pray for one another, challenge one another to be godly in your marriages, and even confront one another when necessary.

Counseling

If, after analyzing your marriage, you identify some rather significant problems that you're unable to sort through, it might be wise to seek counseling. Perhaps your pastor can give you the insight you need. Or maybe he can refer you to a Christian counselor in the area with the skills and experience to help you work through your struggles.

Money Issues

Who can forget that immortal song of the '70s that went "Money, money, money, money...MONEY"? Such lyrical genius prompts one to ask, "Where have all the good songwriters gone?"—but we digress.

The issue here is MONEY. Every married couple struggle with that "filthy lucre"—all couples some of the time, and some couples all the time. So here are some wise and practical financial tips that can keep you in the black.

1. Remember it all belongs to God.

Many of our economic troubles and worries begin with the wrong attitude. It's when we embrace a "me, my, mine" mind-set that we tend to become greedy and money-obsessed. According to the Bible (Psalm 24:1; Haggai 2:8), God owns it all. Everything in the whole world is His, including your portfolio and possessions. By keeping this oft-forgotten truth in mind, we tend to be less grabby, more generous, and more thankful. We end up consulting God more often on what to do with the resources that He has given us to manage.

IT COST HOW MUCH?!

One of the primary reasons for marital friction over finances is that men and women often do not have any idea how much things cost for each other: "Eighty-five dollars for makeup?! What for? A lifetime supply?!";"You paid forty dollars for one gallon of paint?! I hope it has gold in it!"

This exercise is intended to help you appreciate the living expenses of your spouse.

What would you guess your wife has to pay for the following:
_____ A pair of pantyhose
_____ A bottle of top-quality fingernail polish
_____ A name-brand leather purse
_____ A nice, basic black evening gown
_____ A bra and panties set

What would you estimate your husband would have to pay for the following:
_____ A ticket to a professional sporting event
_____ A good, name-brand cordless drill
_____ Four new tires on his car
_____ A bucket of balls at the driving range
_____ A fly-fishing rod and reel

2. Make a budget.

Sit down with your spouse and a pad of paper. Write down all your income on one side. (That generally doesn't take long!) On the other side list your current monthly expenses. (Hint: It helps to keep receipts and write down every expenditure for a month or two so that you can accurately track where your money is going.) Once you have a clear sense of your cash flow and how much you are spending in various categories (mortgage, groceries, personal care items, subscriptions, loans, prescriptions, entertainment, etc.), then you'll have a clearer understanding of why there always seems to be too much month at the end of the money. Or you may finally see why your credit card balance seems to get larger each month.

3. Decide what your financial priorities and needs really are.

Begin with the absolute necessities—tithe and offerings, taxes, loans, basic living expenses (food, shelter, clothing). Ask yourself some hard questions. Can you really afford to spend $250/month on clothing? Everyone would like to spend that much (or more), but the reality is you may not be able to do that on your current income (and fulfill your other obligations). Should you be giving more than $25/month to support your church? What if every member family gave only that much? Are your lofty car payments on that late-model import causing you to forgo saving money, or worse, are they pressuring you into higher consumer debt? Yes, it's hard to discipline yourself to set aside $100/month for emergency savings or retirement, but down the road don't you think you're going to need that money?

4. Set goals.

Many of our financial difficulties are due to the fact that we have no long-term goals. When there's no agreed-upon sense of "This is what we're trying to achieve financially," our use of money becomes impulsive and erratic. It's important for couples to talk about money, to look down the road (as much as possible) and try to foresee opportunities as well as dangers. If both of you had braces as kids, and now your seven-year-old is also snaggletoothed, the chances are good little Pat is going to need to see the orthodontist in the not-so-distant future. A wise couple will begin planning ahead for such possibilities. In the same way, if you both want a cabin on the lake, keeping that big dream in the forefront of your minds can give you the discipline to say no to little unnecessary daily purchases.

5. Think give, save, spend.

Leave it to the real pros to worry about market volatility and long-term global economics. You just worry about three concepts: giving, saving, and spending. Give first (Proverbs 3:9–10). If you wait to see what's left over, you'll find that there is *never* anything left over. Honor God from the first part of your wealth. Save second. It doesn't have to be a huge amount, but you'll be amazed how quickly your money will grow if you are faithful to set aside a little bit every month. One day you'll be so glad you did this. Spend third. Stay within your budget. Be disciplined. Resist the first urge to buy. On nonessential purchases, adopt the overnight rule. Sleep on it. Pray about it. Oftentimes you'll find the next day that that "must-have" item is not so necessary after all.

6. Designate a financial "point person."

There's an old saying: "When everybody's in charge, nobody's in charge." This is certainly true in the area of family finances. If she's paying bills one month, but he's trying to reconcile the bank statement, and she has the checkbook, life becomes chaotic and the source of much friction. (Ever been struck in the forehead by a pocket calculator launched from the kitchen?) One person (either husband or wife, but should be the person who is the most financially astute) should balance the checkbook and keep the financial records in order. He or she can keep the spouse updated on a day-by-day or week-by-week basis.

7. Consult a certified financial planner.

When your car is in sad shape, unless you're a whiz mechanic, you take it to the shop. When your golf swing goes to the dogs, you consult the club pro. Speaking of dogs, when your pet is sick, we're guessing you seek medical attention promptly. We are quick to seek and get help—until we get to this area of personal finance. Why? It's probably pride. But if you're in financial hot water, get over your pride and make an appointment ASAP to see a trained professional who can help you sort through the intricacies of financial goal setting and budgeting. There is absolutely no shame in this; in fact, there's a great deal of wisdom in recognizing you need counsel.

Getting Out of Debt

Those who've been there know how awful it is. Few feelings are worse. The result is long-term misery. No, we're not talking about having season tickets for one of the professional sports teams in Philadelphia. We're talking about being deeply in debt.

What can you do to avoid this terrible condition? Here are seven practical, down-to-earth thoughts:

1. Pray.

Our mandate is to glorify God in whatever we do. . .and certainly that includes how we handle finances. If "all things were created by him and for him" (Colossians 1:16), then even our money is from God and for God. The point? God cares about your financial situation. He cares what you do with your money. So consult Him about it—on everything from earning, to saving, to giving, to spending. . .to getting out (and staying out) of debt.

2. See a financial adviser/counselor.

This is a wise practice for anyone—including those who are not currently in debt. Consulting an expert can save you future headaches. You'll come up with a sensible plan that, if followed, will eventually result in economic prosperity, not disaster. Certainly if you're already in financial trouble, you need to see someone who's been trained to help folks in your situation. And don't despair, lots of couples, in far worse shape than you, have—with God's help—turned things around. Call and make an appointment today.

3. Utilize books by Christian financial experts.

The North American church is blessed to have ministries like Christian Financial Concepts (Larry Burkett's group) and Ronald Blue & Co. that exist to help Christians learn to be good stewards of God's resources. Every couple or family ought to have at least one basic book or workbook by these wise advisers. Written in an easy-to-understand style, these materials are ideal for personal or small-group use.

4. Understand the mystery of debt.

Analysts have studied debt-ridden couples extensively over the last decade or two and gained some profound insights into this phenomenon. What they have concluded (and we are thrilled to be the ones to announce this important finding) is this:

> "Debt is the result of spending more money than one receives, and doing so over a long period of time."

That's it, folks, in a nutshell. No rocket science here. Which means the way to get OUT of debt is basically to spend less than you make, and keep doing so for a long time.

5. Trust God for financial discipline and self-control.

It's tough to reverse bad financial habits. If you're an impulsive person by nature, it's not easy to say no to those consuming desires to "BUY! BUY! BUY!" But you CAN do it. "The fruit of the Spirit is. . .self-control" (Galatians 5:22–23). God has given us a "spirit of. . .self-discipline" (2 Timothy 1:7). In short, you're going to need supernatural help in your battle for financial health, and according to the Bible, God has already provided it!

6. Embrace a simpler lifestyle.

We live in the most consumptive era in perhaps the most materialistic culture in the history of the human race. No wonder we struggle with wanting to acquire more and more things (and no wonder personal bankruptcies are at an all-time high)! It takes an iron will and real guts to go against the flow of society. Take a look at who your friends are. If you are "running with" a well-to-do crowd, if all your acquaintances and neighbors are living affluent, upscale lives, it will be very difficult to avoid the age-old temptation of trying to "keep up with the Joneses." Books like the bestselling Tightwad Gazette series serve as an excellent intro to the simplicity movement.

7. Develop new habits.

So much of our unhealthy spending is due to unconscious, ingrained habits. Many couples have found victory over unnecessary spending by doing some basic things like. . .

- Refusing to peruse mail-order catalogs and newspaper advertisements. These glossy appeals only whet our appetites for more and more stuff.

- Turning off the TV. Have you ever stopped to think that every single commercial is nothing more than an attempt to cause you to be dissatisfied with the belongings you already have and to entice you to replace your old stuff (clothes, cars, jewelry, etc.) with that which is "new and improved"? If you turn it off, advertisers can't make you disenchanted!

- Stay out of the mall. The research is conclusive. The more time you spend in stores, the more money you will spend. Everything about the mall (layout, music, colors, lighting) is designed to put you in an optimal buying mood. Your only hope? To avoid putting yourself in the place where the merchants can lull and woo you.

Talking about These and Other Issues

Picking one's way through all the money problems and sexual issues of marriage can be like navigating a proverbial minefield. One false step and BOOM! Wounded psyches and hurt feelings all over the place! What a mess!

What's the solution? Well, there are no easy answers, but the best precaution is to talk. *Not* talking never solved anything!

Here are some helpful "clues for the clueless" for talking about complicated issues:

Talk proactively.

By this we mean talk in advance. Don't wait until problems become huge. At the first sign of trouble—better yet, *before* there is any indication of a problem—sit down and discuss what's happening in your marriage. Review your finances together. Project what expenses might be looming out there in the not-so-distant future. Have frequent "sexual checkups." (No, this is not where you play doctor with your spouse, though maybe that's not such a bad idea now and then!) Ask yourself and each other, "How are we doing in this area? Are we frustrated? Fulfilled? Healthy? Honoring God? Do we like the direction we are moving as a couple in the areas of money and sex?"

Talk extensively.

BAD

She: "Honey, I think this book on marriage is brilliant. It's maybe the most profound collection of wisdom (other than the Bible, of course!) ever printed. And it says here that we should 'talk proactively' about potential problems. Let's do that."

He: "Okay. How 'bout this? It's 6:58 right now. I've got to run to the convenience store and get some chips before the game starts. It'll just take a minute. How 'bout you ride with me, and that way we could have our discussion before the 7:05 kickoff?"

GOOD

She: "Honey, I'm thinking it might be good for us to spend some time talking about some issues in our marriage."

He: "You're right. It's been a whole month since we had a substantive conversation. How about we get a sitter and go away for the whole day on Saturday."

The point? Snippets of irregular conversation in passing, while not a bad thing, won't suffice to really deal with issues in marriage. You need to carve out some bigger chunks of time to address and solve potential problems.

Talk regularly.

Marriage is like a garden. Good, healthy gardens are maintained daily. Their owners don't just decide to pull weeds or fertilize or spray for bugs once a season or every other year. They regularly and routinely monitor what's going on. They're constantly evaluating and assessing what's needed in order to get the best results. In the same way, your marital relationship needs regular, constant upkeep. Make it your habit to watch over your marriage. Be vigilant. Talk all the time.

Talk clearly.

Mark Twain once quipped, "The difference between the right word and almost the right word is like the difference between lightning and a lightning bug." How true that is. It's important to work at making yourself understood.

The potential for miscommunication is always present, and when discussing delicate, complicated, thorny issues like money and sex, we are somehow even more prone to misinterpret or be misunderstood. Since what we *mean* and even what we *say* are not always what the other person *hears*, we have to labor to ensure that we've heard and been heard accurately.

When you discuss tough issues like these, ask a lot of clarifying questions. This is a great way for underlying misunderstandings to surface. As always, make it your goal to speak the truth in love (Ephesians 4:15).

Talk carefully.

Like few other issues, conversations about money and sex can often make us feel very vulnerable, and thus highly defensive. If we're not careful, one or two poorly chosen words can sabotage an entire discussion (e.g., "Baby, I love you. I think you're the most gorgeous, the sexiest, the most enthralling woman on the planet. That's why I crave you. I want to be with you. I'm hungry for you! So...why do you have to be so *stinking frigid*?!") Pray before you have one of these frank marital conversations. Ask God to give each of you the grace to speak gently and tactfully. Measure your words. Don't be in a rush. Watch your tone. Remember, the goal is to come away from this discussion more unified and more in love than you were before. If you sense at the outset that you're in a cranky, belligerent, "who cares?!" mood, don't even attempt to have a constructive discussion. You won't, if that's your attitude. You'd be better off to go watch TV, fold some clothes, or mow the grass.

9

COMMUNICATION TIPS

Arguments (Fighting Fair, What to Never Say in an Argument)

CONFLICT IS UNAVOIDABLE

Even the most loving couples have conflicts. When fallen, unique, quirky people share life, there will *always* be disagreements. The only way to completely escape arguments in this life is to live alone in a tree house in the Brazilian rain forest. (Reader's note: Most of these tree houses are leased through the year 2028.) Get comfortable with the idea that conflict is an everyday fact of life. The point? Couples who quarrel are entirely normal.

TAKE THE INITIATIVE

Unless you're a regular guest on the *Jerry Springer Show*, you probably detest conflict. In fact, your natural tendency may be to avoid conflict at all costs. Perhaps with your spouse you pretend everything is okay (even when it's not). But "if it is possible, as far as it depends on *you*, live at peace with everyone" (Romans 12:18, emphasis added). Matthew 5:23–24 echoes this idea. In short, the conflict ball is in your court.

LEARN TO LISTEN

Granted, working through a disagreement is not "fun." Who wants to bring up and slog through an unpleasant issue? But the experience of millions of healthy couples is that if you honestly talk things out and listen—really listen—to each other, you'll gain understanding, new perspectives, and a richer relationship. That's a great thing worth pursuing, whatever the cost!

REMEMBER THE GOAL

Lots of people approach conflict not as a problem to be solved, but as a battle to be won. If you don't believe this, consider the military terminology we often use to describe our spats. He prepares to "win at all costs" and elects to "take no prisoners," while she decides, if necessary, to "go nuclear." (Note: This is a sure sign we've allowed the situation to become overheated and hyperemotional.) Think about this tendency: What good is it to win an argument if, in the process, you alienate and/or destroy your mate? When couples stop trying to crush each other in brutal verbal battles and start trying to build a deeper relationship based on understanding and respect, they're on the right track.

IT'S NEVER TOO LATE TO LEARN THE ART OF CONFLICT RESOLUTION

A lot of newlyweds (and older couples, too!) are downright miserable because they have never learned to resolve conflict. Somewhere, somehow, they bought into the crazy idea that "tying the knot," having lots of sex, and pooling their resources and incomes would ensure that they live happily ever after. Surprise! It doesn't work that way.

Marriage is a breeding ground for tension. Only those couples who are willing to sit down face-to-face and hash through conflicts will know the wonders of true marital intimacy.

RULES FOR FAIR FIGHTING

1. If you find yourself extremely emotional, declare a short time-out to give yourself the opportunity to cool down and prayerfully examine your attitudes, motives, etc. Go back and read through this list.
2. Make sure you are yielded to the lordship of Jesus Christ.
3. Seek the filling of the Holy Spirit (Ephesians 5:18), and pray that the fruit of the Spirit (Galatians 5:22–23) might mark your words and actions.
4. Make a commitment to truthfulness and tenderness (Ephesians 4:15, 25).
5. Adopt a "whatever it takes" attitude, a 100 percent approach toward conflict resolution rather than the typical 50/50 rationale that is willing to go only to a certain point and then shuts down.
6. Remember that ultimately the glory of God is at stake in your marriage (Ephesians 5:32).

7. Consider if the issue at hand is really worth arguing over (Proverbs 17:14). Are you just being ornery and looking to pick a fight? Are you wanting to "kick the dog" after a bad day—and viewing your spouse as "the dog"?

8. Select an appropriate time and place for your conversation (where you won't be rushed and/or interrupted). In the checkout line at Walmart? NOT a good place. In your bedroom after the kids are asleep? Wise choice.

9. Agree to stick to the issue at hand (no bringing up old, past events or failures).

10. Avoid statements like "you always" or "you never" or "you should" (this is a condescending statement). Get rid of the phrase "I can't" (this almost always means "I won't").

11. Stick to the issue at hand; DO NOT resort to personal attack.

12. Use "I" statements rather than "you" statements ("*I* feel angry because you cleaned those flounder in the kitchen sink right after *I* cleaned it" rather than "*You* make me want to throw up because *you* are such an insensitive slob, *you* selfish pig!").

13. Do not violate these rules, even if your spouse does. Remind him/her of these agreed-on principles.

14. Humbly admit your own contribution to the problem. Swallow your pride and apologize when and where appropriate.

15. Resist the urge to mind read, pout, clam up, yell, walk away, etc. (See "Communication Killers" on page 142) Resolve to "stay in the ring" until the issue is settled or until both parties agree to call a truce until the conversation can be constructively concluded.

16. Agree upon "out-of-bounds" topics (those issues that have historically proven to be too hurtful or that have already been discussed—obesity, in-laws, etc.).

17. Ask for clarity where you do not understand certain feelings or statements.

18. Practice active/reflective. (See "Seven Tips to Good Communication.")

19. See the conflict as a problem to be resolved to the satisfaction of both teammates, not as a war to be won by one of two opposing teams.
20. Consider your mate as God's instrument in your life, one through whom God may be speaking to you (Proverbs 12:1).

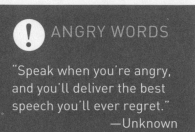

WHAT ABOUT WHEN YOU CAN'T AGREE? In a perfect world, we'd resolve every single conflict with tears of joy and hugs all around. But we don't live in a perfect world. Sometimes you can't find common ground. And that's okay. The mistake many married folks make is to cave in against their better judgment. Generally, the pushier person with the stronger personality wins. It's not good to be stubborn. But it's not healthy to be a doormat either.

Communication Killers

There are techniques and skills that can enhance communication between mates. And there are also practices and habits that can launch an interpersonal Cold War between husband and wife.

Here are ten certified communication killers:

1. Negative body language. Marital experts agree that the following actions are NOT good: not directly facing your mate; folding your arms in a disapproving, closed-off manner; scowling angrily; rolling your eyes in a condescending way; clucking your tongue (in contempt, as if to say, "Well, DUH!").

2. Failing to fully listen. Watch out for "the glassy stare." Beware of looking "through" the person because you are deep in thought about something else. Avoid the male tendency of trying to "kill two birds with one stone" (e.g., do your taxes *and* listen to your wife's account of the devastating phone argument she just had with her mother).

WHAT'S IN A NAME?

These pet names will build up your spouse and marriage:

Darling
Honey
Baby
Sweetie
Precious
Angel
Dear
Beautiful/Handsome
Cutie Pie
Sugar Booger

These names are NOT recommended in addressing your spouse:

Mr. Moron
Brainless Betty
Airhead
Nincompoop
Fatso
Dolt Man
Leona Helmsley
King/Queen of the Land
of Stupid

3. Withdrawing. **Withdrawing can be literal (storming dramatically out of the room) or metaphysical (retreating into your inner self, where you fantasize about being stranded on a desert island with Cindy Crawford or Harrison Ford). Either way, it's not healthy or wise.**

4. Changing the subject. This communicates disinterest, insensitivity, or cowardice. And, hey, who wants THAT epitaph? HERE LIES GLADYS KREBNER: DISINTERESTED, INSENSITIVE, COWARDLY WIFE OF ARNIE KREBNER.

5. Clamming up or pouting. **Some folks use this technique to punish their spouses. If you know your spouse *really* wants to talk about a subject, what better way to get to them than by refusing to engage? This is really immature, and it is the conversational equivalent to pouring gasoline on a fire. Or worse, you may eventually train your spouse not to give a rip about trying to engage you in conversation.**

6. Losing control. Want to make a bad situation worse? Eager to propel your relationship into a critical state where you'll have no choice but to spend hundreds of dollars for a marital referee (commonly known as a professional counselor)? Here's what to do: scream so loudly that you rupture your vocal cords (and your spouse's eardrums); slam a door with enough force to cause glass breakage in the china cabinet three rooms away; punch through the Sheetrock; or hurl sharp objects or small pets at your spouse.

7. Overblowing everything. Let's take a vote. How many readers feel eager and excited about entering these "conversations":

- "Are we going to discuss THIS SAME STUPID SUBJECT fourteen hours a day for the rest of our earthly lives?!"
- "I knew you'd say NO. You always have and you always will! Why must you torment me so?! Why must you make my life so painful that the flames of rejection lick all about my wounded soul. . ." (blah, blah, blah). In short, avoid exaggerating and making ridiculous generalizations.

8. Attempting to mind read and/or psychoanalyze. This is the spouse who's read one too many books on counseling. Rather than merely listening, he/she feels the need to diagnose and explain every feeling and action. This isn't communication; it's an emotional autopsy! Who wants to sign up for that?

9. Seeking peace at any cost/caving in. Also known as the "Yes, dear!" or "Whatever" strategy, this close cousin to "withdrawing" is a wimpish technique that would rather brush issues under the rug than expend the mental and emotional energy needed to actually work through a problem. In time, these undiscussed, unresolved issues will come back with a vengeance. Down the road, it can truly be horrifying. Think *Night of the Living Dead* set in the context of a marriage.

10. Turning up the volume on the TV.
Nothing communicates "I don't care" more than gluing your gaze to the boob tube. The more you stare at the so-called idiot box, the less you will communicate with your spouse. Which is preferable: that you know all the plots to every episode of the forgettable TV series *Veronica's Closet*, or that you know what your spouse is thinking, feeling, dreaming, and planning?

MISCOMMUNICATION

Her: (weeping and shaking) "And . . .so. . .the. . .test. . .came. . .back . . .positive. . . ." (thirty seconds of hysterical sobbing) "I. . .just. . . don't. . .know. . .what. . .to. . .do!"

Him: (not looking up from sports page) "I totally agree, babe. What's for supper?"

Eight Tips for Better Communication

Be Spirit-filled!
Can you imagine the difference if your marital conversations were marked by the qualities listed in Galatians 5:22–23?

1. Be careful!
Ask God for the discernment to know when to speak and when to keep your mouth shut. Also, for the conviction to put the brakes on when the conversation drifts into questionable territory.

2. Be attentive and sensitive!
Listen to what your spouse is saying. Recognize that sometimes people aren't able to articulate what they're truly thinking or feeling. You may have to probe some and work to really "hear" what's actually being said beneath the words.

3. Be quiet!
Someone has noted that God gave us two ears and only one mouth, meaning we ought to listen twice as much as we speak. Don't hog the conversation. Ask questions, then sit back. You might even learn something!

4. Be honest!

We are called to always speak the truth in love—Ephesians 4:15. Don't give in to the temptation to "not bring up" important (but delicate) issues.

5. Be loving!

It's been said that we ought not to speak hard words to someone until we have at least prayed for that person and at best wept for that individual. Don't pummel your spouse (or anyone else) with raw truth. (Such bluntness can be a very thinly veiled form of verbal abuse). Always wrap your words in compassion and gentleness. Remember the Golden Rule here!

6. Be wise!

The tongue, like fire or dynamite, is an instrument that can be used for great good or for great evil. Once a word leaves your lips, you can never get it back.

7. Be encouraging!

Seek always to edify and build others up. This is that old idea of "If you can't say something nice, don't say anything at all." The world is filled with too much negative talk. Make it your goal to be a positive voice.

 STICKS AND STONES

Popular author and speaker Charlie Shedd (*Letters to Karen, Letters to Phillip*) tells the story of a young husband who got angry and, in the heat of passion, told his insecure wife, "I never did like your freckles!"

Clearly, a single hurtful comment can cause long-term devastation!

WHAT'S MY SCORE?

Give yourself a grade (A, B, C, D, or F) in each of the following categories.
Then try to imagine how your spouse might grade you.

CATEGORY	MY GRADE	HOW MY SPOUSE WOULD GRADE ME
Taking the initiative in conversation	_____	_____
Using basic conversational skills	_____	_____
Being skilled at drawing others out	_____	_____
Being willing to converse beyond a superficial level	_____	_____
Showing wisdom regarding when to initiate deeper conversations	_____	_____
Listening attentively	_____	_____
Resisting the urge to interrupt	_____	_____
Thinking before speaking	_____	_____
Being open with feelings	_____	_____
Being honest	_____	_____
Avoiding obnoxious communication habits (talking too much, changing the subject, dumping loads of advice on someone who's hurting, etc.)	_____	_____

cont. ->

CATEGORY	MY GRADE	HOW MY SPOUSE WOULD GRADE ME
Being straightforward (i.e., refusing to resort to manipulative techniques)	_____	_____
Being objective	_____	_____
Making myself understood	_____	_____
Being willing to say hard but truthful things	_____	_____
Sticking to the issue at hand in a conflict	_____	_____
Going the extra mile to resolve conflict	_____	_____
Standing up for legitimate rights	_____	_____

The Lost Art of Listening

Hearing is easy. It is the passive reception of "what" is being said—words and facts. *Listening* is a different matter altogether. Anyone who's ever tried listening—*really* listening—knows that it is one of the hardest skills to master in all the world.

Listening involves actively seeking to understand the "why?" behind the what. Good listeners hear the words, but they also go behind the words to the deeper (and often hidden) feelings of the sender. Rather than "thinking of how to respond" while the other party is talking, or prescribing a quick solution or simplistic answer the moment the other person pauses to take a breath, a good listener seeks to empathize and identify with the other party. He asks questions to clarify. She wants more than anything else to understand.

A LISTENING EXERCISE. . .

Take turns completing the following statement:

"I felt _____ when _____."

Important reminders:
- Avoid "you" statements that will put your mate on the defensive (e.g., "You are spending us straight into the poor house!"). By making "I" statements (e.g., "I feel worried when you make purchases while our checking account is so low."), you share information and feelings in a less threatening way.
- When you are talking, your goal is to be honest and sensitive.
- When you are listening, you want to do so with your full attention, energy, and focus.

Instructions:
1. Wife, go first.
2. Husband, humble yourself! Resist the urge to defend, explain, rationalize, justify, or attack. Make understanding your goal. Listen actively. Put yourself in her shoes. Empathize. Ask questions to clarify. Respect your wife's feelings. Restate them. Honor her.

LET'S TALK

"In an era of increasingly fragile marriages, a couple's ability to communicate is the single most important contributor to a stable and satisfying marriage."

—George Gallup

3. Husband, go last. Resist the urge to hurt, wound, or get even. Complete the statement above in such a gentle way that your wife will listen, learn, and understand you. Give her the opportunity to reflect back to you what she has heard you say.
4. Discuss the exercise. What did you learn about listening? About the power of feedback? About yourself?
5. Kiss and make up (and do whatever else comes naturally!).

Knowing How to Forgive and How to Receive Forgiveness

A whimsical calendar states (regarding marital love):
> *"The torch of love is lit in the kitchen."*

This may be true (whatever it means), but we have also observed that when it comes to marriage,
> *"The white-hot coals of disgust have been known to blaze at the dinner table. . ."*

Leading to incidents in which
> *"The leaping flames of anger rage in the bedroom. . ."*

Culminating in situations in which
> *"The smoldering wick of bitterness glows fiercely from the living room"* (where the husband lies sleeping on the couch).

In less poetic words (and this is a profound insight, so grab a highlighter!),
> *"Husbands and wives get ticked off at each other."*

It can happen in any situation for any number of reasons. He's being an insensitive doofus; she's being overly sensitive. He's in a nasty humor; she's

PMSing. They're both thinking about themselves. Neither is particularly concerned about pleasing God.

Mix up those kinds of attitudes with a careless remark or two. Throw in a thoughtless action and WHAM! Torches *are* being lit, but they have nothing to do with love!

Some things to remember when you've got an uncivil war raging on the home front:

1. Life is way too short (Psalm 39:4) to spend it fighting with the ones you love.

2. We can't be right with God if we're not right with the people God has sovereignly placed in our lives.

    This is a MAJOR theme in the first epistle of John! Also 1 Peter 3:7 gives special warnings to husbands, implying that when they are inconsiderate and insensitive to their wives, their prayers will be ineffective!

3. Nobody is truly "innocent," and therefore nobody has the right to be condescending or unforgiving to another.

    Over and over the New Testament links our obligation to forgive with the fact that God, in Christ, has forgiven us. In short, we're ALL sinners! There's no room for a "holier than thou" attitude in marriage.

4. Forgiveness isn't a feeling; it's a choice.

    What is it we "owe" others and that they "owe" us? To love and think of them as much as we love and think of ourselves (Mark 12:33), and to treat them as we want to be treated (Matthew 7:12). In a moral/spiritual sense, when we *fail* to do this (i.e., to give them what we "owe" them), we become indebted to them.

FORGIVE

"Bear with each other and forgive one another if any of you has a grievance against someone. Forgive as the Lord forgave you."

Colossians 3:13

Forgiveness is the Christlike decision to cancel such debts. It's wiping the slate clean. It's refusing to maintain a mental list of all the ways someone has wronged you. This quality is the primary difference in marriages that sparkle and marriages that hurt just to look at.

Bitterness is the opposite decision: to keep track of every debt. It's the sick choice to keep hanging on to and rehashing old wrongs in order to fan the glowing embers of resentment. (Note: Did you know the word *resentment* originally meant in Latin to "feel again"?!) Allowing this in a relationship is like choosing Chinese water torture (only instead of water, you're opting for the slow, destructive drip, drip, drip of acid).

NO GRUDGES ALLOWED

"A good marriage is the union of two forgivers."

—Ruth Bell Graham

Fifty-Two Ways to Say "I Love You"

It is arguably the world's worst cliché. It is overused. It can often seem trite. Everyone who has ever loved, who has felt his or her heart filled with great depths of passion and commitment, knows how inadequate the phrase "I love you" can seem. Woody Allen, in one of his earlier movies, had a love-struck character frantically grasping for new ways to express such deep affection. "I lurve you!" he exclaimed. "I lorve you!"

Lurve. Lorve. Love. Whatever you want to call it, the most important thing is to express it. And maybe it's time for us to realize that those three familiar words aren't enough. Could we describe Niagara Falls or the Grand Canyon in only three words?

The next few pages are an attempt to give you some new and different but also highly practical ways to convey to your beloved the deep mysteries of your heart.

SAYING "I LOVE YOU!" IN WORDS

- Buy (or borrow from the library) a book of love poetry (the Brownings, Shakespeare, etc.). Spend an evening reciting these sonnets and odes to your spouse.
- Read portions of the biblical Song of Solomon to your beloved. (Note: This portion of scripture contains some pretty juicy stuff!)
- Write a love song or ballad and practice it/learn it on the guitar or piano. Then sing it to your sweetie. Or if you can't carry a tune in the proverbial bushel basket, ask a talented friend (or hire a professional singer/musician) to record it on audiotape for you.
- Write a passionate love letter to your mate and mail it to him/her at his/her place of business.
- Leave a mushy note in your spouse's briefcase or lunch bag.
- Write a few choice endearing words on the bathroom mirror using lipstick or soap.
- Make a long list of all the things you admire and appreciate about your husband/wife. Present it to him/her.
- When the timing is right, whisper some romantic (maybe even sexy?!) words in his/her ear.
- Ask about his/her day. Then listen with everything you've got.
- Learn to say "I love you" in different foreign languages.
- Using a cassette recorder, get different friends, neighbors, colleagues, or church members to say a few words about your

HOW DO I LOVE THEE?

"How do I love thee? Let me count the ways. I love thee to the depth and breadth and height my soul can reach."
—Elizabeth Barrett Browning, *Sonnets from the Portugese*

spouse—why he/she is special.

- Before the next meal time, arrange for the whole family to give short speeches about why he/she is special. Give a standing ovation after each oratory.

- Take an entire evening and reminisce before a roaring fire (or in front of a raging air conditioner in the summer!) about your relational history. Look back through scrapbooks and old pictures.

HOW TO SAY "I LOVE YOU" IN SIX FOREIGN LANGUAGES

Turkish: "Say-nee say-vee-yor-um"   Italian: "Tee a-moe."
Dutch: "Ick how von yow."   Swahili: "Mee-mee na-pen-da vway"
French: "Zjuh tem"   Russian: "Ya ta-byah loo-bloo"

SAYING "I LOVE YOU!" IN ACTIONS

- Make it your goal to begin and end each day with a warm hug and a tender kiss.
- Pick that one chore that your honey absolutely detests, and do it for him/her this week without any warning.
- Call during the day for no other reason than to remind your mate of your love.
- Men, be chivalrous! Open doors for your wife; pull her chair out (but not out from underneath her). Stand up when she enters or leaves a room. Make your sons do the same.
- Turn off the TV or stop whatever you're doing and give him/her your full attention every time you engage in conversation.
- Pray with your spouse daily.
- Men, demand that your kids show respect to your wife/their mother.
- Clean out or wash his/her vehicle.

- Get together (preferably in private!) and take off all your clothes. See what happens.
- Make it your goal to always have fresh breath.
- Be sensitive! Don't track up the freshly mopped floor! Don't scoop up all his carefully organized stacks of papers into one jumbled pile!
- Sit down together and come up with some short- and long-term marital goals.
- Sit down with a financial planner and develop a workable, realistic plan for your family's financial future. Caring for your family in this way (by having adequate insurance, etc.) is a strong nonverbal message of love and concern.

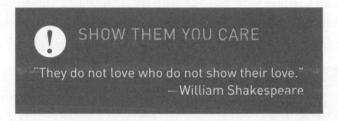

! SHOW THEM YOU CARE

"They do not love who do not show their love."
—William Shakespeare

SAYING "I LOVE YOU!" IN SURPRISES

- Kidnap your spouse for a night on the town (or maybe even an overnight getaway at a nice hotel or nearby bed-and-breakfast). Pack for him or her, make all the arrangements, and then, without warning, just take your spouse away.
- Give your beloved an all-out, lengthy, sensual massage, caressing that warm skin and feeling those firm muscles under your trembling, aching fingers FILLED WITH YEARNING—ahem, er, yes, um, let's see, moving right along to other possible surprises. . . .
- Get up early and bring your beloved breakfast in bed (or just coffee, if he/she is not a big breakfast-eater-type person).
- Fix his/her all-time favorite meal.
- Fix/mend (without being asked) that messed-up possession that is

driving him/her up the wall.

- Guys, call her up from the office and ask her several days in advance for a real live date (always preferred over a fake dead date).
- Invite him/her home for a romantic interlude during lunch (if you know what we mean, and we're betting you do!).
- Set up a lunch party for her and all her girlfriends.
- Arrange a golf (or fishing or tennis or bowling) outing for him and his best three buddies.
- On his/her next birthday, plan and throw a surprise party.
- Ladies, buy some sexy lingerie and surprise him that night.
- Go with her (willingly, even gladly) to that meeting or art show opening (or whatever it is that you normally avoid).
- Take a bubble bath together with romantic music and candlelight. (Safety tips: Don't set the CD player too close to the tub! And wait at least thirty minutes after eating before you go into the water.)

 KEEP THE FIRE BURNIN'

"Once you marry, you're not to stop all the attentive responses. They're to increase. It's a continual attitude. Keeping the romance alive is a matter of little daily acts. It means that your spouse is on your mind, not just 'Oh no, it's Valentine's Day again. I better go buy something and do something romantic.'"

—H. Norman Wright, in *Virtue* magazine

SAYING "I LOVE YOU!" WITH GIFTS

- Save your pocket change over the next few weeks or months and buy her/him several favorite magazines or that new novel by his/her favorite author.
- Make something with your own hands that would mean the world to your spouse—a carving, a personalized lamp, a restored antique, a wall hanging, a scrapbook, etc. Take your time and do it right.

- Bring her flowers for absolutely no reason at all. Deliver them yourself to her office or walk in the door with them after work. (Note: You get *major* bonus points if you do this when you're not already in the doghouse.)
- Send him/her a card (funny or racy, it doesn't matter).
- Have a really nice picture made of yourself. Give large and small copies that he/she can both frame and put in the old wallet/pocketbook.
- Give the gift of learning. Pay for enrollment in a class she's always wanted to take (cake decorating, computers, etc.); write a check for the registration fee for that conference he's been wanting to attend; spring for lessons for acquiring some new skill (e.g., juggling or tap dancing).
- Buy his/her favorite all-time movie and wrap it up in a gift bag with popcorn and candy.
- Give him tickets to the big game or to the auto show.
- Give her tickets to that touring Broadway show.
- Have a small, inexpensive plaque made and engraved with a personal note of affirmation/affection.
- Splurge for a bottle of nonalcoholic champagne.

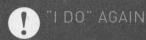

"I DO" AGAIN

"On our tenth anniversary my husband secretly arranged to have friends and family gather at our church. We were, so I was led to believe, just stopping by the church to pick up a forgotten item on our way out of town for a romantic weekend.

"Once inside the building, my husband handed me a dozen roses and walked me into the sanctuary past dozens of our loved ones (and our two boys). We walked up the aisle to the altar where the pastor who had married us ten years before led us in renewing our vows.

"Restating those promises to each other was so meaningful after ten years of marriage. When we concluded our brief ceremony, there wasn't a dry eye in the house. We proceeded to the weekend of our lives!"

—Cindi, Ruston, Louisiana

- Give a gift certificate to a store he/she really loves but rarely gets to shop in.
- Abstain from some of your own normal expenditures (soft drinks, newspapers, gum, etc.) and use this money instead to purchase something he/she's been wanting but has been unable to afford (new golf shoes, a handbag, a small decorator item, etc.).

THE CIRCLE OF LOVE

Love is always active and creative. Creativity, in turn, requires time, effort, and energy. Time, effort, and energy expended to express love for a spouse generate an ever-deepening affection. Thus, real love never stops; it's an endless circle!

Communicating Your Wishes, Hopes, and Dreams

The Amazing Kreskin aside, no human has the ability to read his or her spouse's mind. (And such powers wouldn't really be an asset to your marriage anyway, since you'd keep having to replace all the bent spoons in your silverware drawer.)

The point is, ladies, if you don't do a little asking and probing, you may never know that your husband secretly dreams of quitting his high-paying

TRUE LOVE

"Love is patient, love is kind. It does not envy, it does not boast, it is not proud. It does not dishonor others, it is not self-seeking, it is not easily angered, it keeps no record of wrongs. Love does not delight in evil but rejoices with the truth. It always protects, always trusts, always hopes, always trusts, always hopes, always perseveres. Love never fails."

1 Corinthians 13:4–8

corporate job and opening his own earthworm farm out in the country. By the same token, gentlemen, wouldn't *you* feel stupid to get ten (or twenty!) years into marriage only to discover that your wife privately wishes you'd make passionate love to her more often?

All this to say, it's important for couples to be more overt and intentional in sharing with each other their wishes, hopes, and dreams.

Here are easy ways to do that:

1. An annual conference

Lots of successful, happy couples make it a priority to get away for a weekend every year. Oh sure, they relax and eat out at nice restaurants (and get frisky!), but they also set aside some extended time during the weekend to think long-term. Together they develop and/or revise their marital mission statement (a document that spells out their lifelong goals and dreams). A weekend like this is kind of a marital "checkup." It serves a visionary, "big picture" purpose. By asking questions like "How are we doing financially, spiritually, emotionally, etc.? Where are we going?" couples are able to chart a clear course, ensuring that they don't just drift through life aimlessly.

2. Quarterly confabs

A leisurely day away or a lengthy evening date (over a nice dinner) serves the purpose of helping couples "check their course in the middle of the stream." The goal here is

 SHARE YOUR DREAMS

Unless you become proactive, making the intentional effort to talk about important "big picture" hopes and dreams, your days (and ultimately your *life*) will be filled with reacting to urgent (but often trivial) issues like meetings and deadlines.

not to talk about the nitty-gritty urgencies at home or the office (e.g., "We really need new tires on the van," or "I'm worried about that deal with Smegley Consulting"). Rather, this is where you discuss bigger issues (parenting, retirement, the kids' spiritual condition, annual goals, etc.).

3. Weekly consults

An hour on Sunday afternoon or evening is a good occasion to look back at the previous week (to evaluate, to celebrate successes, to learn from mistakes) as well as to look ahead at what's looming. Some (with older children) choose to make this a "family conference" where everyone brings his/her appointment book or personal calendar and the goal is to make sure everyone is on the same page.

4. Daily catch-ups

The breakfast table is a perfect time to *preview* the day's goals for each family member. Ask questions like

- What are you going to do today?
- What do you hope to accomplish before your head hits the pillow tonight?
- What did you not get done yesterday that you need to do today?

Set aside fifteen minutes a day (right after work/just before supper or even during dinner) where you talk about what happened since you were last together. Work at making this a time when the family looks forward to sharing and hearing what is going on.

Making a Decision Together

Sometimes decisions are no big deal...

> Him: "Where would like to eat tonight?"
> Her: "I don't care. You choose."
> Him: "You REALLY don't care?"
> Her: "I don't. It doesn't matter. Whatever."
> Him: "You don't have a preference?"
> Her: "OH, FOR PETE'S SAKE, WOULD YOU PICK A RESTAURANT!"

At other times, more is at stake...

> Him: "It's a great offer, babe. It's like a 30 percent increase in salary."
> Her: "Yeah, but look at all we'd be leaving."
> Him: "I know. A great church. Lots of friends. Family close by."
> Her: "So what should we do?"
> Him: "I have absolutely no idea."

In times like these, several possibilities exist:

- You can do nothing until finally the circumstances of life force you one way or the other (the wimpy way out, and a method that may cause you to miss some great blessings).
- You can flip a coin (not recommended for big decisions).
- You can try the Tarzan method (he does whatever *he* wants, and "Jane" just has to get used to the idea. Not recommended EVER!).

Here's some better counsel for making the tough decisions together:

1. *Gather all the facts.* Knowledge is power, they say. It never hurts to know all the details.

2. *Talk it out.* Thinking out loud is a great way to achieve new insights. Let your partner vent. Grant the freedom to say anything (even off-the-wall, off-base statements). Such brainstorming sessions yield lots of cuckoo ideas, but occasionally you see a decision from an important new perspective.

3. *Defer to each other's strengths.* If she has a degree in architecture, it might be wise to let her have the larger say in which home is built better. If he's been breaking down engines and putting them back together since he was four, let him lead in the choosing of a new car.

4. *Listen.* Remember that your perspective is limited. God has blessed you with a spouse who can be a great asset (but not if you're unwilling to hear what he/she has to say).

5. *Sit on it.* Don't be rash. Don't rush! Tell that salesperson who pressures you with statements like "This offer is for today only!" to hang it from his beak. Sleeping on a decision, mulling it over, can save you from an impulsive and foolish choice with long-term consequences.

6. *Pray about it.* Ask God to lead you. Ask Him to give you both a sense (the same sense!) of what to do. Solicit the prayers of others. Beware of situations where one partner feels strongly one way, and the other has an opposite impression.

7. *Watch for pettiness.* Some folks use big decisions as an occasion to "get back" at their mate for a previous wrong. For instance, she knows he really wants that red truck (and deep down, she knows he *needs* a more reliable vehicle), but because she's still ticked about his insensitivity earlier in the week, she blocks the deal by saying, "I just don't feel right about it." Don't be petty or stubborn! Be big in

these kinds of situations.

8. *Gather wise counsel.* It was Woodrow Wilson who said, "I not only use all the brains I have, but all I can borrow." You can never go wrong by gathering good and godly counsel.

 CAN YOU HEAR ME?

"It is impossible to overemphasize the immense need humans have to be really listened to, to be taken seriously, to be understood. No one can develop freely in this world and find a full life without feeling understood by at least one person."
—Paul Tournier

10

IN-LAWS

Engagement

Remember the classic play *Romeo and Juliet*? In case you dozed through English Lit. class in high school, the basic plot was this: He and she were star-crossed lovers from families that, in Shakespearean terms, "hated each other's guts." Romeo's family viewed her as "that shrew in need of taming." And her dad, oddly nicknamed "Puck," went insane, causing him to wash his hands over and over while muttering to himself: "Should I let them be a couple, or should I not let them be a couple? THAT is the question."

In short, then, R and J's relationship never really got off the ground because of family interference. Imagine that—a play from the late 1700s about future in-law problems! That bard, he was one sharp cookie.

Marriage therapists today agree that "in-law problems" are one of the top reasons couples seek counseling. In other words, all those mother-in-law jokes exist for a reason!

WELCOME TO THE FAMILY

While it's true that couples are to "leave" their families of origin and "cleave" to one another (forming a new, distinct family unit), it's also true that you don't just marry a person; you marry into a family. For the rest of your lives (unless you and your spouse happen to be lifelong scientists aboard the space station), you will be interacting with each other's parents and siblings. The point? Make it your goal to get off to a good start.

Ten Questions/Statements for Engaged Couples to Think about and Discuss

1. Take turns describing the ultimate, ideal in-law relationship.
2. Take turns describing how you think your parents and your significant other's parents view the ideal in-law relationship.
3. Several Bible passages (Genesis 2:24; Matthew 19:5–6; Mark 10:7–8; and Ephesians 5:31) mention the aspect of newlyweds

"leaving and cleaving." What does this mean to you?

4. How do each of your parents feel about the upcoming marriage?
5. Speculate on what you think your future in-laws say and think about you in their most honest, unguarded moments.
6. Give some specific examples of parents showing interest and concern to their married children. Give some specific examples of parents meddling and interfering in the lives of their married children.
7. What thing(s) do your partner's parents do that you like and/or admire?
8. What thing(s) do your partner's parents do that bug you?
9. How might it demonstrate honor to your parents and in-laws to sit down with them sometime before your wedding and ask their advice on what makes a successful marriage? What counsel do you think they might give?
10. What is your biggest fear as you contemplate your future in-law relationships?

 A LIFE OF SUFFERING?

Did you hear about the woman who slept with her glasses on? She wanted to be able to clearly see her son-in-law suffering in her dreams.

Newlyweds

Marital Truth #247: In the first months and years of marriage, couples establish patterns of relating that, for good or ill, will likely be with them for life.

What are the implications of this truth for in-law relationships? Simple—if you get off to a warm, positive start with your in-laws, the odds are good you'll enjoy a long-term cordial relationship. On the other hand, if your first year of marriage is filled with frequent telephone and face-to-face arguments with your mother-in-law—about everything from oven settings to career decisions, this does not bode well for your future.

Here are four bits of in-law wisdom learned (the hard way!) by several marriage veterans:

1. The "Five Hundred Mile" Rule

Most experts agree that newlyweds who enjoy a healthy bit of geographical distance fare better in the in-law department than those couples who live near their parents. The distance forces couples to lean on the

UNDERSTAND WHAT'S NORMAL

Parents have a hard time letting go of their children. Even when they know their little darling is marrying a sweet, caring Christian, there is still that lingering feeling that "No one is good enough for my son/daughter!" or "No one will love him/her like we do." Try to understand these normal parental instincts. But more than that, do everything in your power to convince your future in-laws that you are the best thing to ever happen to their child.

Lord and each other (and not depend unhealthily on parents). It also prevents parents with intrusive tendencies from butting into a newlywed couple's business. If at all possible, create space during the first year or two. After that, you can be in the same county and you'll be less susceptible to in-law meddling.

2. The "Don't Share Marital Dirty Laundry with Your Folks!" Policy

You have a marital spat. Or a knock-down-drag-out. You're fuming. He's a jerk. She's a selfish brat. Do yourself a favor. DON'T call your mom and/or dad and vent. You may get things off your chest and feel better. But parents have a hard time "flushing" these kinds of conversations. They will (consciously or not) keep a mental list of how that son/daughter-in-law is not being a good spouse. Human nature is that over time we suppress and/or forget bad memories. Unless they have to do with our in-laws!

3. The "Blood Is Thicker Than Water" Dictum

It's December 23rd, say, and you're home for the holidays (after an exhausting drive). Mom announces she *really* wants you two to participate in the annual Christmas Eve tradition of rousing Christmas caroling with the church choir. You'd both sooner submit to a root canal without anesthesia. Instead of letting your spouse (the "in-law") be the party pooper, you need to be the one to say no. Your parents will be ticked off, but they'll forgive you sometime over the next three months. They wouldn't forgive your spouse for three *years* (if then).

4. The "Stand Up for Your Spouse" Law

A parent inappropriately criticizes your spouse (i.e., their son/daughter-in-law). Or they are cool. Or cold. Or downright rude. You must not ignore this. Gently and lovingly confront your mom/dad and let it be known that you will not stand idly by and allow this kind of mistreatment. If you do nothing, your parent(s) will be emboldened to step up the attack, and your spouse will feel betrayed and abandoned.

Some in-law questions for newlyweds:

1. How will you respond if and when your parents say something negative about your spouse?
2. How and where will you spend your first Thanksgiving and Christmas holidays?
3. What have you done in the last month to show appreciation and love to your parent(s)?
4. What specific things have you done so far during your first year of marriage to try to build goodwill and a good relationship with your in-laws?
5. Read Genesis 26:34–27:46. What principles (good or bad) for in-law relationships do you see here?
6. Read Exodus 18:13–24. What principles (good or bad) for in-law relationships do you see here?
7. Read the book of Ruth. What principles (good or bad) for in-law relationships do you see here?
8. What emotional ties with your parents interfere with your relationship with your beloved?
9. Would you consider borrowing money from either set of parents? Why or why not?
10. What are the pluses and minuses of getting into financial deals with parents?

Midlife

We all have people in our lives with whom a good relationship seems unimaginable. Maybe for you it's an in-law who's been giving you grief for years. Perhaps as you contemplate that relationship, you see numerous barriers to intimacy and countless reasons why you could never be close.

If so, you need to revisit the Old Testament book of Ruth. The story takes place during the time of the judges, one of the bleakest periods of Israel's history (Ruth 1:1; Judges 21:25). In it, Ruth and her mother-in-law, Naomi, forge a remarkable relationship following the deaths of their husbands.

There were a lot of human reasons their relationship should not have worked—the in-law factor; a possible clash of class (some scholars believe Naomi's husband came from a prominent family in Bethlehem); an age barrier (the women were at least a generation apart); cultural differences (Ruth was a Moabite, Naomi an Israelite); religious obstacles (Ruth's people worshipped the god Chemosh, a repulsive fact to a monotheistic Jew like Naomi); the pressure of economic hardships (remember this story took place during a time of extreme drought); the tragedy syndrome (both women were reeling from the sudden deaths of their husbands).

And yet even with all these barriers and obstacles, the relationship between Ruth and Naomi didn't just work—it soared! Why?

1. Time (1:4)

Ruth and Naomi had a lengthy history together in Moab—at least ten years. Time can be either a friend or a foe. If you faithfully keep doing the right things to improve and deepen a relationship, time is your greatest ally. Good relationships take time to build.

2. Authentic faith (1:6, 8–9, 13, 16–17, 20–21; 2:20)

Naomi talked freely about the Lord in conversations with Ruth—her belief in Him, her bitterness at Him. She clearly believed in His power, sovereignty, and goodness. How many people do you know who, if their spouse died, would choose to live with their mother-in-law?! Clearly there was something different about Naomi. Though she was far from perfect, Naomi modeled a godly life for her daughter-in-law. And Ruth was drawn to her and her God, and away from her pagan roots.

3. Unselfishness (1:7–14; 2:18)

Naomi might have considered her desperate situation as an aged widow and said, "Please stay with me and care for me. I'm old. I need you." She didn't. She thought instead about the well-being of her daughter-in-law. Ruth acted the same way—unselfishly caring for her mother-in-law, working hard to bring her food, once they got back to Israel.

4. Kindness (1:8, 19–21; 2:11; 3:1)

The kindness present in the relationship between Naomi and Ruth was an ongoing, reliable thing. Ruth showed kindness (2:2) when she announced she would go and gather grain for the two of them. Naomi showed kindness to Ruth (3:1) when she announced her intention to find a husband for her daughter-in-law. They looked for concrete and practical ways to bless each other and help each other and then did them. Repeated acts of kindness are the building blocks God can use to turn improbable relationships into incredible blessings.

5. Commitment (1:14–18)

Many people don't know that the classic statement "Where you go, I will go. . . ," which is so often quoted at weddings, was originally uttered by a daughter-in-law who was physically clinging to her mother-in-law! It's an amazing scene of commitment—the almost stubborn refusal to walk away from someone. Only this kind of devotion can salvage difficult relationships.

PRIORITIES

"There is one source of energy behind every interpersonal act: either a priority interest in ourselves or a priority interest in others."
—Larry Crabb, Anderson, Indiana

Parenting

Raising children is tougher than ever. . .meaning we need all the help we can get. Often one of the best resources is the kids' grandparents (i.e., your own folks and your in-laws). Why are they ideal?

- They're eager. Most grandparents can't wait to get their hands on their grandkids.
- They're experienced. They've already done the parenting thing. And they must have done something right—after all, they reared you and your sweetheart! Your kids need all that wisdom your parents have gleaned through the years.
- They're (usually) available. This is one of the great advantages to retirement—many elderly couples find they have the time and money to travel.

So it's imperative to get your parents and your in-laws on the team. Communicate your desire to involve them in the upbringing of your children. But be ready for three typical trouble spots:

1. Temptations to take advantage

"Well, Granddaddy's always saying how much he wants to see the twins, so I'm sure he wouldn't mind if I dropped them off at his house every afternoon for the next month." Or you arrive at your in-laws, unpack the car, get the kids settled, and announce, "Y'all don't mind if we go out for the evening, do you?" These kinds of expectations can create major ill will. Don't use your parents or in-laws. Don't presume on the relationship. That's insensitive and a quick way to create conflict. It's okay to ask for help, but be careful that you don't abuse the relationship.

2. Disagreements over child rearing

It's inevitable. Grandma will feed the kid(s) something you don't approve of, or Gramps will take them somewhere that makes you nervous. You have no choice but to gently address the situation. No matter how tactful you are, odds are good you'll hurt feelings and create some weirdness. But here's the real key: It's always wise for each spouse to confront his or her own parents in these types of situations. In other words, if it's HIS MOM who is handling the kids in a way you don't like, HE needs to be the one to address it with her. Parents forgive and forget with their own sons/daughters far more quickly than they do with the sons/daughters-in-law.

3. Grandparent rivalry and jealousy

Sometimes the different sets of grandparents can get into subtle (or not-so-subtle) competitions for the grandchildren's affections. Your parents want to see the kids at Christmas, but so do his folks. Sometimes the children prefer and gravitate toward one set of grandparents. This dynamic can make for some really weird encounters (i.e., your in-laws resent YOU because your kids prefer your parents to them). All you can do is try to be fair, make sure each set of grandparents has equal time, and be super careful to "talk up" your in-laws (and never "run them down").

 JUST LIKE DAD

A young woman, upon her engagement, went to her mother and said, "I've found a man just like Father!"

Her mother replied, "So what do you want from me, sympathy?"

Retirement

The golden years. The twilight of life. Whatever label you choose, there's something mysteriously profound about the final decades of life. It's during this dramatic phase of life that many people make peace with their parents and in-laws. . .or not.

It was Erma Bombeck who, years ago, eloquently described this time as when the child becomes the parent, and the parent becomes the child. In other words, the roles slowly reverse, and grown children often end up caring for their aging parents and in-laws.

A few random thoughts:

- *Schedule as many visits as possible.*

  Life is both unpredictable and brief. You and your spouse will probably have plenty of regrets when your folks are gone. Don't accentuate your grief by realizing you should have made more attempts to see them.

- *Make the most of your times together.*

  Don't spend your time arguing over petty issues. Talk. Communicate about meaningful things. Express your love and appreciation. Do thoughtful acts of kindness. Live in such a way that you will have few regrets after they're gone.

- *Sacrifice.*

  It costs a lot to raise a child—time, money, energy, effort, emotion. In short, both you and your spouse likely have much for which to be thankful. Show honor to your parents by being willing to care for them in the same costly, sacrificial ways they cared for you. Don't be like so many baby boomers who have parked their parents in nursing homes and all but forgotten them. Cherish them. Hold them in high regard. Do everything in your power to make their final years comfortable, happy, and special.

ENJOY THEM WHILE YOU CAN

Look at the morning obituary page. Calculate the average age of death. It will probably be in the sixties or seventies (let's say it's sixty-nine). Now consider the age of your parents and your spouse's folks. Let's say they're sixty-five. This means, based on the law of averages, they may have only four years of earthly life left. Consider if you only see them three times a year, this means for all practical purposes, you might have as few as twelve visits left with them. The point here is not to be morbid, or to depress you, but to help you adjust your priorities.

GO DEEPER

"One of my best all-time memories happened in the fall of 1988 when my aging in-laws paid a visit in their travel trailer. We met them at a nearby state park, just the four of us, and spent the weekend sitting around a campfire telling stories and talking about our lives. It was fascinating to hear about their childhood experiences, and those conversations gave me a deeper understanding and a greater appreciation for them."

—C. Witmer, Atlanta, Georgia

11

MARRIAGE SAVERS
AND BREAKERS

Becoming a Better Friend

THE VALUE OF FRIENDSHIP

Chum. Pal. Bosom buddy. Best friend. Do those words give you a warm, fuzzy kind of feeling? They probably remind you of someone who was or still is very important in your life. You can let your mind wander and remember things you did together years ago or maybe just last week. A little smile might be tugging at the corners of your mouth as you recall a special conversation or adventure with that special friend.

Hopefully, your spouse is the first person who comes to mind when you think of your best friend. This chum and pal (alias husband or wife) listens to your good news and is happy with you. He or she also offers understanding when you're down and encouragement when you're discouraged. And he or she tries not to say, "I told you so," when you do something really stupid.

Having your spouse and best friend all rolled up into one person is a wonderful bonus of marriage!

PEP-UP ACTIVITIES

An undernourished body becomes weak and listless. The same thing can happen to an undernourished friendship. This weak friendship may not die, but it will be pretty lifeless and just sort of limp along. When this happens to the friendship of a husband and wife, a big dose of "pep-up" activities may be in order. Take one or two of these each day and you won't need to call the friendship doctor:

> ### FRUITLESS SEARCH
>
> "Don't look for perfection in your spouse. You won't find it, and it's just as well. Living with a saint could be very tiresome."
> —Abigail Van Buren

- *Talk, talk, talk:* Think back to your childhood friend. You yakked away about anything and everything, no secrets between you. Talk to your spouse about the joys, disappointments, fears, and happiness in your life. Share things you've read or heard that will interest him or her. No secrets— unless they involve planning surprise parties or secret gifts!

- *Listen, listen, listen:* The flip side of talking is listening. Really listen to your spouse with your ears and mind open and your mouth closed until he or she is finished talking. Be appreciative of what your spouse is saying verbally and through body language and respond accordingly. Sometimes a hug or a joyous dance around the room is a lot more expressive than words.
- *Be adventurous:* One of the best things about having a childhood buddy was having great adventures (and misadventures) together. Having adventures with your "spouse buddy" can be great fun, too. Go exploring—try new foods, take long walks together, learn something new. Dare to be silly. Laughing with each other is marvelous fun.
- *Mind your manners:* If your spouse is your best friend, then he or she deserves your best manners. Common courtesy goes a long way toward smoothing out the bumps and ruts of marriage. When there is a disagreement or disappointment, calm discussion usually goes a lot further than slammed doors, clanging pans, and yelling matches. Mom and Miss Manners will be so proud of you, and your spouse will think you are the best friend in the world.

COMPROMISE

When two people get married, they each bring along their own life experiences, likes, and dislikes. Even though your spouse is your best friend, you probably have differing opinions on many things. Actually, it would be very boring to agree on everything!

You need to learn the wisdom of compromise, for it's better to bend a little than to break.

Think back to your childhood friend. When he wanted to play baseball and you wanted to play video games, what did you do? You probably decided to compromise (even though you didn't know the word existed). Maybe you played baseball for a while and then played some video games. Each of you gave a bit, and each of you felt happy about the solution.

The same principle still works with your "best friend" spouse. If you are a cheery morning person and your spouse is more of a grumbly bear, keep the chatter to a minimum. If your spouse wants to go to an auto show and your heart is set on a garden display, compromise and spend some time at each place. Compromise leads to harmony and a better understanding of each other.

YOUR FIVE OR SIX SPOUSES!

Now don't get excited! Polygamy is not being endorsed or promoted. Living in harmony with one spouse takes a lot of work; just imagine what it would be like to live with five or six! Yipes!

If you and your spouse are married for a number of years, you may have five or six different spouses—but they will all be the same person. This isn't really as confusing as it sounds. As we age and have life experiences, we change.

Unless you are newlyweds, you and your spouse are not the same as when you were married. Your spouse doesn't go through a metamorphosis and become a completely different person every seven years, but both of you change because of circumstances and growth.

Some of the causes for change can be...

- *Age:* Everyone changes and hopefully matures as they age. Things that were superimportant when they were younger may not be so paramount anymore.
- *Children:* Being a parent gives a whole new perspective on every aspect of life.
- *Life Experiences:* These include career, friendships, hobbies, and education. Unfortunately, accidents and illnesses are also often a part of life experiences.

Most of these changes are good—they make life interesting, challenging, and fulfilling. So enjoy each one of your spouses—what a lot of best friends!

THE VERY BEST FRIEND

The very best friend you and your spouse can have in your home is Christ. Invite Him to be the center of your marriage and the relationship you have with each other.

To learn how to be a friend to your spouse, use Jesus as a role model. He is the Friend of you and your spouse who exemplifies how to be a true friend. Jesus' friendship is giving, loving, and unselfish. In John 15:12–14, Jesus says, "Love each other as I have loved you. Greater love has no one than this: to lay down one's life for one's friends. You are my friends."

GOOD MARRIAGE

Definition of a good marriage: "It's a spend-the-night party with your best friend for the rest of your life. That's the way my wife and I live, taking seriously being each other's best friend—putting away distractions, giving each other total attention, being willing to communicate, being willing to learn to be a good listener. Giving your time is a great act of love. If you do that, you are always attentive enough to know what the other person is needing."

—Ron Davidson, Atlanta, Georgia

Simplifying Your Life

K. I. S. S.

It really stands for "Keep It Super Simple!"

"It" can be anything that is causing anxiety or stress or turning you into a crosspatch. That catchy little slogan can help you refocus and think about what is really important. Following the sign's advice puts situations into a better perspective and frees you up to enjoy what you're doing.

Keeping things simple for you and your spouse may mean having casual get-togethers with friends instead of full-course dinners. It can mean just spending time together instead or running hither and yon. Or it can mean doing without a lot of "stuff" that needs washing, polishing, or special care, but is seldom used or even noticed. You know what needs simplifying in your life.

LEARN TO SAY NO

"How many dozen cookies can you make for the bake sale?" "We should have a big party for all the relatives." "You would make the perfect soccer coach!" "All my friends have it; I really need it."

Do you and your spouse feel as if you are on everyone's hit list? Are there so many demands on your time and energy that you feel like skipping town without leaving a forwarding address? Is your life filled with busyness? When someone asks you to do something, does your mouth say, "Yes," while your brain is screaming, "No! No! No!"

Friends, neighbors, church members, and family may all be clamoring for your attention and help. They are not being nasty or unreasonable; they just know that you usually come through. If you and your spouse find yourselves in this predicament, then it's time to teach your mouth to follow the directions of your brain and learn to say no.

Turning down a request may be difficult to do at first, especially if it's for something you've "always done." But in order to simplify your life and spend more quality time with your spouse, you need to say no to at least half of the things you are asked to do.

Once you have made a decision to say no to a request, stick with it. Be friendly but firm. Whether or not you explain why you are refusing is your personal choice. The person doing the asking may be disappointed or surprised at your refusal, but he or she probably won't become angry. And there is no reason for you to feel guilty about turning them down—even if they are fellow church members.

It is not God-pleasing if you are so busy helping everyone else that you have no time or energy for your spouse.

CLUTTER CAN BE COSTLY

A cluttered home can lead to frustration, wasted time, and unnecessary expense. When there is too much "stuff" or nothing is gotten rid of, it's very difficult to find that important letter, the keys, or even the remote. Frustration levels and blood pressures shoot up as a frantic search takes place. Precious time is wasted looking under, over, and through things. Hopefully the searched-for item is finally located.

But sometimes the thing being sought seems to have disappeared into thin air. This causes even more problems and anxiety. Deadlines may be missed and appointments canceled. Perhaps a replacement needs to be purchased, adding unexpected expenses to the whole mess.

You and your spouse may live in a neat, orderly home with everything in its place but still have a cluttered life. And a cluttered life can be quite damaging to a marriage. When your married life is full of outside commitments, causes, and "things," you may experience an overwhelming sense of being pulled in many directions.

A comedian quipped, "You know you're middle-aged when you don't care where your wife [husband] goes, as long as you don't have to go with her [him]." The comment was meant to be funny, but it is really a sad commentary on many marriages. When too much time and energy is spent doing lots of "things," you may have very little of either to give to your spouse. That can lead to feelings of isolation and separation. If left unchecked, this busyness can even cause spouses to drift apart and lead to the breakup of a marriage.

When your life becomes too cluttered, it's time to do some clearing out. You need to pick and choose your priorities and simplify your life in the process.

SIMPLIFICATION PLAN

Sorting out and uncluttering your life may not be easy, especially if there are children in your family. Simplification will not happen overnight and it may be a difficult process, but it is not impossible. Here are a few hints to get you and your spouse started on a simplification plan:

- *Pray about it.* Lay all your concerns and hopes before the Lord and trust Him to guide you to make good decisions.
- *Have a family meeting.* This meeting may only involve you and your spouse, but if you have children, involve the older ones in the discussion. Sit down together and take time to really talk about ways of making family life simpler and less harried.
- *Make a list.* Have each family member list everything that takes up his or her time and energy outside of normal living activities. This list could include sports teams, hobbies, meetings, committees, and other commitments.
- *Prioritize.* Now have each person prioritize his or her list, giving number one to the most enjoyable or important.
- *Eliminate.* Discuss how to eliminate or minimize involvement in the least important things on the list. You may want to start with one or two things and slowly, over time, eliminate or modify some of the others.
- *Consolidate.* Are there some things on your list that are very similar to those on your spouse's list? Try spending time doing them together, instead of each one doing his or her own thing.

Just like surgery, the original cut may be quite painful. But as time goes by, you probably will not miss what was eliminated. In fact, you may wonder why you ever spent so much time and energy on it in the first place.

COMMON COURTESY

Any lasting relationship is built on true friendship. Your spouse is deserving of the courtesies and kindnesses you give to your friends.

Career and Marriage

WHAT IS MEANT BY A CAREER?

Let's face it, unless you and your spouse are independently wealthy or inherited millions from a long-lost relative, at least one of you needs to work and earn money. It puts food on the table, clothes on your back, and provides for the necessities and maybe a few luxuries.

What exactly is a career? Webster defines it this way: "a profession for which one trains and which is undertaken as a permanent calling; a field for or pursuit of consecutive progressive achievement."

You and your spouse may have spent years of training for your careers, or you may have been an apprentice and learned hands-on. Whatever one does for a living is his or her career. Ideally, your career provides you with satisfaction and enjoyment.

As my dad so often said, "Working is good for you, and getting paid for your work is even better. When you also like what you're doing—well, that's wonderful."

BLASTOFF?

Careers, like rockets, don't always take off on schedule. The key is to keep working on the engines.

A TRICKY BALANCE

Unless you married at a young age, you and your spouse probably both were working before your marriage. You may have even met each other at work or in college preparing for your life's career.

Being an unmarried working person allowed you to put most of your time and energy into pursuing your career. As long as she was fed, the cat didn't mind if you came home late or dragged home a briefcase full of work and spent weekends finishing projects.

But then you got married and your spouse was not as tolerant as the cat. Too many late nights and long weekends working to catch up or get ahead were not appreciated. Your spouse wants more of your time, energy, and attention.

This can become a very tricky balancing act between marriage and career. If you and your spouse are both working, it gets even trickier.

DUAL CAREERS

Dual careers means dual incomes, but it can also mean dual headaches and arguments.

Do you and your spouse have some of these common complaints of others in a dual-career marriage? "We don't have time to really talk." "Most of our time is taken up with work." "He [she] spends so much time and energy on his [her] career that there's none left for me."

Did you notice that time is mentioned in all of these complaints? Of all the gifts God gives us, the one that is distributed absolutely equally is the daily gift of time. It is the same amount and passes at the same rate as it has since creation.

So instead of complaining about lack of time, think of ways to use time more efficiently. Then you and your spouse will have extra free time to enjoy each other's company.

ADDING KIDS TO THE MIX

You thought having dual careers was difficult? Well, add a kid or two to the mix and things can really get crazy!

If you and your spouse both have careers and are planning to have children or already have children, you probably need to answer some hard and serious questions. Ideally, these questions should be discussed and decisions made before the first child comes into the family.

Find a quiet place, pray for guidance, and then honestly discuss these questions. Listen to each other carefully as each of you expresses your opinions and feelings.

1. Will both of us keep working full-time?
2. Who will care for the children?
3. How can we manage the household, children, and careers?
4. What can we do to keep our marriage important and vibrant?
5. Should one of us work part-time or quit?
6. Should one of us work at home?
7. How can we decide who will work part-time or quit?

There are no wrong or right answers. You and your spouse are unique, and you need to answer these questions in a way that fits into your needs and lifestyle. Any decision you make now will change and be rearranged as children grow up and circumstances change.

GIVING IN WITHOUT GIVING UP

The number-one cause of arguments, fights, and bad feelings in marriage is money. Spouses quarrel over the making of money and the spending of money. Career choices also come under fire because money is earned by following one's chosen career. Hard decisions concerning careers and marriage are bound to come up. Here are some common dilemmas involving marriage and careers.

- Both of you have exciting careers. One of you is offered a great advancement, but it involves moving to another state. Whose career will take precedence?
- Your spouse makes a good salary and has regular advancements in his or her career. But there is no joy or enthusiasm in doing the job. He or she wants to quit and follow his or her dreams into an entirely different field that pays quite a bit less.
- Before your first child is born, you decide that one of you will be a stay-at-home parent while the child is young.
- Your spouse loves his or her new job, but it involves long hours and frequent business trips.

Perhaps you and your spouse have faced some of these dilemmas or are involved in something similar right now. Unfortunately, sometimes it seems that spouses need to make a choice about which is more important—marriage or career. Don't fall into that trap; it shouldn't even be considered an option.

Whenever a major career choice arises, pray with your spouse, asking God to guide your discussions and decisions. Then talk to each other about every aspect of the situation. Actually write it down in two lists, one of the advantages of change and another of the disadvantages.

When everything has been discussed and analyzed, practice the art of giving in without giving up. In other words, compromise. Then there won't be a winner or loser. It will be a win-win situation, and your marriage will be strengthened.

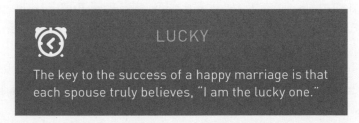

LUCKY

The key to the success of a happy marriage is that each spouse truly believes, "I am the lucky one."

Vacation Ideas

WHY TAKE VACATIONS?

> *"Vacation" is a marvelous, magical word to me.*
> *It conjures up visions of mountains, sun, and sea.*
> *It promises freedom from the daily routine*
> *And whispers of wonderful places to be seen.*

No matter how much you love your home, your job, and your family, everyone needs to take periodic vacations.

- Vacations give you a break from your daily routine.
- They are a time to rejuvenate and gain a new perspective on things.
- Vacations are a time to be alone with your spouse.
- Vacations give you something to dream about as you plan and anticipate them.
- Vacations give you wonderful [or wacky] memories to think, talk, and laugh about.

Even Jesus took time out from His busy schedule to rest and be quiet. "After he [Jesus] had dismissed them, he went up on a mountainside by himself" (Matthew 14:23).

MINI-VACATIONS

It may seem impossible for you and your spouse to find a large chunk of time and/or money to spend on a vacation. Not to worry. Take several mini-vacations during the year.

These mini-vacations can be long weekends or day trips. One rule—break out of your daily routine and do something entirely different. Here's a short list of ideas:

- Weekend package at a nearby hotel or resort
- Day in the city visiting museums, zoos, art galleries, etc.
- Day in the country having a picnic, walking in the woods
- Touring nearby historical sites or state parks
- Camping in a state park or campground

This list can be adapted to your area and what is available. Look in a state tourist book or a large newspaper to find interesting events and festivals in your area.

WATER VACATION

"My husband and I decided a romantic mini-vacation was needed, and the very best place for this getaway was that wonderful little place by the lake. We had spent a week there ten years earlier and had so much fun. We hopped into the car and hit the road—only a two-hour drive in the country. Our first clue of impending disaster should have been the nonexistent countryside—everything was houses, stores, and traffic. Things didn't improve. The lake was closed to the public, and the perfect little cottage looked pretty seedy. We decided to stay overnight anyway—bad decision. In the middle of the night we awakened to the sound of running water. A driving rain had found a huge crack under the door and we had a stream running through the room. We wanted a place *by* the lake, not *in* the lake! We survived and even laughed about it, but we learned to always call ahead before we set out on a marvelous adventure."

—Jeanette, Chicago, Illinois

VISITING RELATIVES

Because we lived seven hundred miles from our families, our vacations for the first ten years of our marriage were always spent with relatives. Maybe you and your spouse are in a similar situation. There are definite advantages to vacationing with relatives, such as fewer expenses, seeing people you haven't seen in a while, and being in a familiar setting. If you have children, it gives them a chance to interact with grandparents, uncles, aunts, and cousins.

Some of the disadvantages can be lack of privacy, little time to relax, and being unable to do things you and your spouse want to do. A week to ten days is usually a long enough visit. After that, you get on one another's nerves.

ROMANTIC VACATIONS

Absolutely no children, pets, friends, or relatives are allowed on a romantic vacation! This is strictly for you and your spouse. Another no-no is talking about work and worries. And *never, never* take along "a little work" to do. How romantic can that be? This is a time for the two of you to be carefree and completely absorbed in each other.

You and your spouse need to decide together where and how you will spend this romantic vacation. If possible, make the vacation at least ten days long. Decide on the type of vacation and the destination at least two months before you plan to go, and then work out all the details. Make airline reservations if you plan to fly and make reservations at hotels or resorts where you will be staying. No vacation is completely goof-proof, but the more planning that goes into it, the better it will be.

Where to go and what to do are entirely up to you and your spouse. It depends on your tastes and your budget. Whatever you decide, make it something very special and wonderful for both of you. Here are some ideas:

- *Cruise:* This can be expensive, but you will be waited on hand and foot—truly treated like royalty. However, this is probably not what you want if you desire to be alone together.
- *Resort in an exotic setting:* This can be Hawaii, the Caribbean, or any other romantic tropical place. Here you can truly be alone together and do what you please.
- *Cabin or cottage:* This could be a rented place in the mountains, by the ocean, or by a lake. It could be rustic or quite modern.

- *Large city:* Stay at a hotel and visit all the wonders of the city. Dine in a different restaurant each day. See plays and attend concerts.

VACATION OF A LIFETIME

This is the ultimate vacation. This is the big one—the one you and your spouse save up for and dream about for years, maybe decades. It is the vacation to end all vacations.

Many times the "Vacation of a Lifetime" means spending a month traveling through Europe, South America, Africa, or Asia. Perhaps it is going to Australia, the "country down under."

Some folks loll about on a South Sea island, and others explore remote parts of the world.

A vacation of a lifetime is a dream that is altered, expanded, and refined over time. And when it finally occurs, every bit of it is photographed and videotaped and it lives on in memories long after you are back home. If you and your spouse have such a dream, try to make it a reality and enjoy every second of it!

12

BUILDING MEMORIES

Birthdays

A RED-LETTER DAY

Everyone, from the age of 2 to 102, likes to be remembered on his or her birthday. This even applies to those folks who say, "Never mind my birthday. It's just another day." Deep down they do want you to "mind."

Birthdays are special because they celebrate an individual, not a season or a holiday. Young children think about their birthdays for weeks before the event. They also give frequent reports on how many days are left until the BIG day and how old they will be. As people get older, some of this enthusiasm diminishes, but birthdays are important at any age.

DO YOU REMEMBER?

Children like to hear about the day they were born and look at pictures of themselves as babies. Married people like to hear about their wedding day from the perspective of friends or relatives. A display of wedding pictures at an anniversary party can stir a lot of memories and stories!

A King or Queen for a Day

Make your spouse's birthday a special event—treat him or her as king or queen for a day. What makes your spouse really happy? Is it dinner in a nice restaurant or a special home-cooked meal served by candlelight? Perhaps doing something "different" will be just the thing—but not so different that your spouse thinks it's weird or feels uncomfortable. Maybe the best celebration is kicking back and having a "lazy" day (busy moms and dads love this). Be creative and have fun. The important thing is to show your love for your spouse by thinking of him or her and what he or she likes.

For children, royal privileges may include choosing a special family outing for the day, such as visiting the zoo, seeing a movie, or picnicking in the park. The "king" or "queen" can also choose what to wear (within reason) and the menu for their birthday meal, including dessert.

SURPRISE!

Ray had been SO secretive planning Joyce's surprise birthday party. All the guests were asked to park down the street and then sneak in the back door of the family room. Right before the party was scheduled to begin, there was a loud banging on the front door. Ray was pretty annoyed as he went to the door—someone was going to spoil the surprise. When Ray opened the door, he faced two burly policemen saying they had come to look around. A neighbor had reported some suspicious characters sneaking around in the back of the house. Unaware of what was happening at the front door, the guests decided this was the perfect moment to yell, "Surprise!" Fortunately the policemen weren't the "shoot first and ask questions later" sort!

TO PARTY OR NOT TO PARTY

Each family will choose how simple or elaborate, big or small, they want a party to be. Here are some options:

Immediate family: Use the suggestions above to have a fun day with just the immediate family. Cards and small gifts add to the festivities.

Extended family: If you have no children, this could include parents, brothers, and sisters. If you have grown children, include them and their families (they may even treat you to a great dinner). Kids in the family? Then include grandparents, uncles, aunts, and cousins. Parties can be as simple as cake and ice cream or as elaborate as dinner—or anything in between. It depends on the number of people and the age of the birthday person.

Children's party: This can be a party in the home with decorations, games, and simple food, or it can be outside the home in a place that hosts children's parties. The number of guests and their sex depends on the age of the birthday child. Here is a good rule of thumb: 5–6 years: 8–12 guests, boys and girls; 7–8 years: 12–18 guests, all boys or all girls; 9–11 years: 10–15 guests, all boys or all girls.

Milestone parties: Significant milestone years: 16, 21, 40, 65, and any year after 70 are often celebrated with special parties. They can be elaborate dress-up parties in the home or at a restaurant. They can be surprise parties or a party at a theater, sporting event, or some other special place. It should be planned so that the guest of honor is comfortable and has a wonderful time.

Count the Blessings along with the Candles

Take some time during the birthday celebration to reflect on God's presence in the celebrant's life. Remember that God made each person and put him or her into a special family to be loved and cared for. Thank God for all the blessings He gives the birthday person each and every day.

When the "Happy Birthday" song is sung, add this second verse:

> *God's blessings to you,*
> *God's blessings to you,*
> *God's blessings, dear _____,*
> *God's blessings to you.*

Thanksgiving Day

A FAMILY HOLIDAY

Thanksgiving Day is a marvelous holiday. Compared to the commercialism and superhype that accompany all the other holidays, Thanksgiving Day almost seems to be overlooked. Grocery stores have sales on turkeys, cranberries, and sweet potatoes, and a few rows of Thanksgiving cards show up on the card rack, but this is not a big Madison Avenue type of holiday. And that's what makes Thanksgiving Day such a wonderful holiday! There are no Thanksgiving gifts to buy, no decorations to put up, and no round of parties to attend.

Thanksgiving Day is definitely a family holiday—no matter if your family is just the two of you or a large extended family. It is a time to share good food, great talk, memories, and the fun of being together.

Celebration Ideas

If you and your spouse are celebrating Thanksgiving Day by yourselves, share the food preparation. Tell each other why you are thankful that you are husband and wife. And thank God for each other and all the blessings He gives you.

If Thanksgiving Day is celebrated with the extended family, go to a different home each year. You don't need to "go over the river and through the woods" to Grandma's house every Thanksgiving. She will be quite happy to go somewhere else. The host/hostess can provide the turkey (or any other meat) and each guest can bring their favorite Thanksgiving food to share. Oh, what a tasty feast you will have!

By the way, it is not terrible to make reservations at a nice restaurant and have the family dinner there. You can always gather at Aunt Millie's (or Grandma's) afterward for dessert, games, conversation, and whatever else makes the day complete.

Being Truly Thankful

Football, food, and family are wonderful components of Thanksgiving Day, but the top priority is to remember all of God's blessings and to offer a special thanks for them. The scriptures are filled with songs and prayers of thanksgiving. Attend a Thanksgiving worship service with your spouse or your family and join other believers in giving thanks to God.

You and your spouse can read some of the wonderful psalms of thanksgiving to each other. Some of the more familiar ones are Psalms 100, 121, 148, and 150. One of these psalms can also be used as a table prayer.

Everyone can participate in a circle prayer. One person starts the prayer, and then each person, in turn, mentions one thing they are thankful for. When everyone has had a turn, the prayer can be closed by the same person who began it.

Another idea is to make a Thanksgiving poster. Print "Thanks, God" in the center of a large poster board or piece of newsprint. Place the poster and a supply of markers in a prominent location. Each person can write a short phrase telling what he or she is thankful for and sign his or her name. Making a poster each Thanksgiving could become a family tradition.

THANK YOU

"Give thanks to the LORD, for he is good. His love endures forever."
Psalm 136:1

Sharing the Blessings

Thankfulness can be shown by sharing the blessings God gives you. Here are some suggestions for backing up thoughts and prayers of Thanksgiving Day with actions:

- Invite someone who will be alone on Thanksgiving Day to spend the day with you and your family. These people could be widows or widowers, college students far from home, or new immigrants. Think of people in your neighborhood, at work, or at church.

- Volunteer to help serve meals at a homeless shelter or for any agency that prepares a special Thanksgiving dinner for those who need it.

- Take dinner to someone who is housebound or unable to prepare a meal for themselves.

Christmas

STRESS-FREE HOLIDAY

That title surely sounds like a combination of contradictory words—an oxymoron if ever there was one! Unfortunately, Christmas has become the most stressful of all holidays. The buildup begins weeks ahead of time and increases in intensity as December 25th nears. Trying to do EVERYTHING can lead to frustration, short tempers, and large doses of crabbiness.

But Christmas truly can be stress-free with some careful thought and planning. You and your spouse need to decide on two or three Christmas activities that are important to you and then concentrate on them. These could include decorating, baking, family gatherings, gifts, caroling, Christmas pageants or plays, or anything else that is very special to you. Putting your energies into what you really want to do will be fun, exciting, and stress-free.

If you have elementary-age or older children, give them a voice in the decision making. And encourage them to contribute ideas and participate in the chosen activities.

KEEPING CHRIST IN CHRISTMAS

Several years ago the campaign "Keep CHRIST in Christmas" was promoted on billboards, radio, and TV. The idea was to make people really think about the true reason for and meaning of Christmas. The campaign was an attempt to counteract the commercialism of Christmas, with its emphasis on gifts, parties, and Santa. The hope was to bring Christmas back to a religious observance with the focus on the birth of Christ. As you and your spouse plan your Christmas activities, keep Christ in your Christmas. Use an Advent wreath or calendar to anticipate the coming of Christmas. Display a crèche, listen to Christmas carols, and attend Christmas worship services.

GIFTS

One young lady told me that when she and her siblings were growing up, they only received three gifts each because that was how many gifts Jesus got from the wise men. Not a bad idea.

If you have children, read the Christmas story from Luke 2:1–20 aloud to them. Encourage them to participate in Sunday school or church Christmas programs, and invite friends and relatives to attend.

EXPECTATIONS

More people become depressed during the Christmas holidays than at any other time of the year. The main reason for this depression is because of the high expectations they place on themselves, others, and the holiday. These people are determined to have the perfect holiday. When this doesn't happen and they don't have as much fun, get as wonderful gifts, or feel as loved as all the people in the advertisements, depression sets in. Being realistic and not expecting perfection can lead to enjoyment instead of depression.

Cards, Decorations, and Parties

- *Cards:* If you choose to send cards, decide with your spouse on a master list. Do you want to send cards to EVERYONE you've ever known or just to family and special friends? Do you want to send a newsletter, make your own cards, or use commercial cards? There is no right or wrong way; just do what you are comfortable with and enjoy.
- *Decorations:* You and your spouse may need to do some compromising on the decorations if each of you has definite ideas about what's best. You can choose to have a theme tree, display Christmas collections, or be the envy of the neighborhood with an outdoor display. Children love to help decorate. Let them make some decorations to display and put on the tree.
- *Parties:* If you are hosting a party, keep it simple so you and your spouse can enjoy it. A trimming-the-tree party, dessert party, or caroling party could be lots fun. If you plan a full-blown family dinner, use some of the ideas given for Thanksgiving dinners.

The Art of Giving

Gift giving is a big part of the Christmas tradition, and you probably don't want to do away with it. Try to give gifts that are creative and original rather than merely costly. Don't just plop something in a box, wrap it in fancy paper and ribbon, and hope one gift fits all.

When selecting gifts for your spouse, keep in mind his or her interests, hobbies, and passions. This probably won't be too hard to do since most husbands and wives often drop broad hints of what they would like!

It goes without saying that children definitely let you know what they want. To avoid a bad case of the "gimmies," set a limit on the number of gifts the children will receive and tell them what to expect before Christmas morning. This may make them more selective in what they request.

Anniversaries

REMEMBERING

Anniversaries can be observed for any significant event—your first job, your first date with your spouse, or the day you moved into your home. But usually your wedding date is what comes to mind when you think about an anniversary. The day you and your spouse were married marked the beginning of a whole new way of life. Your wedding day was the day when your separate lives were united into a joint life. From that time on, the two of you were a family.

No matter if you were married in a small ceremony with only a few people present or if you had the largest and most lavish wedding in recorded history, the date of that wedding is certainly worth remembering and celebrating!

FIRST THINGS FIRST

When you celebrate your anniversary, put first things first. The most important elements of any wedding anniversary are you and your spouse. After all, there wouldn't be an anniversary if the two of you had never gotten married! How you celebrate is up to the two of you—but DO remember the day and have some sort of celebration.

No matter how busy you are, shut off the TV, the phone, and any other distractions to make some quiet time to be alone with your spouse. If you have kids, ask Grandma to invite them to spend the night or at least a few hours at her house.

Anniversary cards and small gifts can be a part of your celebration, but they are only preludes to the main attraction. That main attraction is your spouse and what makes him or her feel special. Remember what made you fall in love with your spouse in the first place and tell him or her about it. Tell your spouse why you would marry him or her all over again.

Candlelight and Roses OR Hiking Boots and Trails?

You and your spouse can spend your special day in any way that is fun and meaningful to you. Use your imagination and remember some of the things you did when you were dating or try something you've never done before. The only rule is that whatever you decide on, it needs to be enjoyable for both of you.

Perhaps your best celebration is a home-cooked dinner with all your favorite foods. Set the table with the best linens and china. Flowers and candlelight add a romantic touch.

Camping out or discovering new trails for hiking or biking may be the perfect way for you and your spouse to celebrate your anniversary. Or on a more elaborate scale, you can spend a getaway weekend or a vacation for just the two of you at a special place. Whatever works for you is great—go for it!

Every Year Is Special

Your wedding anniversary should be observed in some way. While it is true that every year is special, some years may be more significant and can be observed in a more elaborate manner. In addition to the celebration ideas mentioned above, there are more ideas in the section "Anniversary Parties."

Every anniversary, whether simple or elaborate, should also be a time to remember that God is the third partner in every successful marriage. Thank

Him for being with you every day of your marriage and ask Him to continue to bless your marriage.

A meaningful way to celebrate a "milestone" anniversary is to renew your wedding vows before your friends and family. This is often done at the twenty-fifth, fortieth, or fiftieth anniversary, but you can do it at any year. Talk to your pastor about your plans. He can give you advice and perform a simple ceremony for you.

ANNIVERSARY PARTIES

Freedom of Choice

When it comes to anniversary parties, *almost* anything goes. There are no traditions to follow as there may have been at your wedding. The choice of how to celebrate is entirely up to you and your spouse. Of course, if you decide to celebrate by having a bungee-jumping party, your guest list might be quite short!

The entire party should be planned by you and your spouse together. The goal is to have a great time celebrating your love for each other.

Party Ideas

Maybe you want to have a very small party and just invite each other. But in case you want a few more guests, here are some suggestions:

- *Friends:* These could be friends who were at your wedding or friends who have come into your life since you've been married. You can set up the wedding video or pictures and relive the big day. This can be a casual party at your home or anywhere else you choose. Children can be invited, but it's probably more fun to have adults only.
- *Family:* Family celebrations can include your immediate family or the whole kit and caboodle of relatives. This is a time to invite children. Depending on how long you have been married, these children could include your children and grandchildren. This celebration can be as casual as a picnic or potluck supper. The simpler you keep the party, the more you can enjoy it.

- *Special:* Some years are milestones and call for special celebrations. The twenty-fifth and fiftieth anniversaries are often celebrated with big formal parties in a banquet hall or private room in a restaurant. This is the time to sit back and be the guest at your own party. Depending on your budget, try to invite friends and family, being sure to include the people who were in your wedding party. Display your wedding pictures, and if possible, have someone model your wedding dress.

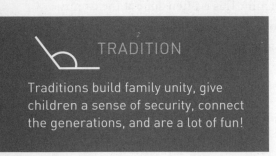

TRADITION

Traditions build family unity, give children a sense of security, connect the generations, and are a lot of fun!

Gift Ideas

WHY GIVE GIFTS?

Gifts tell the recipients that they are special and you want to help them remember the important days in their lives. Gift giving is also beneficial to the giver. It lets the giver express his or her love and admiration for someone in a tangible way. The joy of giving a gift is to see the pleasure it gives the recipient.

GIFT-GIVING OCCASIONS

Birthdays, anniversaries, and Christmas are days that are usually associated with gift giving. But gifts can be given at any time. Sometimes the spontaneous, unexpected gifts are the most fun to give and receive. Here are some times when you might consider giving a small gift:

- *Graduation:* Graduating from high school or college is a significant event.
- *New job:* The first job or a change in jobs is worth noting.
- *New home:* Housewarming gifts are always welcome.
- *Birth of a child:* This is a major event in any family.

MEANINGFUL GIFTS

For a gift to be meaningful, it needs to reflect the interests or needs of the recipient. This makes the recipient know you were really thinking about him or her and not just buying something willy-nilly.

Some of the greatest gifts aren't purchased from a store. They are gifts of your time or talents. Are you a gardener? Give gifts of fruits, vegetables, or flowers to your friends. Do you have a special talent such as woodworking or sewing? Homemade gifts are always extra special because they are one-of-a-kind and a part of yourself is in each one.

The gift of time is priceless. Take time to visit a sick or lonely person. Set aside time to read to a child or to give them a whole day of your undivided attention and do whatever they choose.

No matter what you choose to give someone, keep in mind what would make him or her happy and go from there. Be creative, spontaneous, and have fun!

13

BLENDED FAMILIES

Stir Well

THE HOUSE BLEND

When it comes to families, there are all sorts of shapes and configurations. It's no news flash that the traditional or nuclear family is far outnumbered by family blends today. Whether through divorce, death, adoption, or foster parenting, the family unit today gets a different face with each neighborhood street you pass.

Though there are unique things to be considered in a remarriage and/or reconfiguration of the family, blended families have just as much of a chance at happiness and success as any other family. The key is to understand your challenges and communicate through them.

WHAT CAN HELP US NOW?

For years, Hollywood and television have served as cultural indicators—faithful prophets of coming change. The screen was blending families long before the average viewer caught on to the massive upheaval in the traditional family unit.

The next time you're counseling a divorced coworker at the watercooler, suggesting a weekend of Nick at Nite reruns may not immediately come to mind as good advice. But you may be surprised at the insight and advice one can glean from these forerunner commentaries on the changing American family.

YOU'RE NORMAL

All families have their own challenges because of the particulars of the people in them.

FAMILY AFFAIR

Little Children in a Blended Family

This TV show is an excellent portrayal of a single man raising little ones... who weren't even his own biological offspring. Their unique problems are food for thought for someone considering dating/remarrying in the same genre: single parent raising younger kids. We know

- Little children (ages 2–3) more easily adapt to a remarriage.
- Older children who have established attachment and familiar family patterns have more difficulty coming around to the idea.

And a word of advice to the single parent who may be considering dating or remarrying: make sure your blended family child is as free to communicate with you about their hurts and confusion as Buffy and Jody did with Mr. French! Communication with younger children is essential in helping them to be open with their feelings.

MY THREE SONS

Balancing Sex Role Models for Kids

Here we encounter the joys and sorrows of a parent challenged to rear children without the influence of the opposite sex. A divorced parent often struggles to balance the lack of an influential opposite-sex role model in their children's lives.

Your own personal beefs toward an ex-spouse can transfer negative self-esteem to your children when they consider their sex role. For example, a boy who learns from his mom how rotten a father and husband his dad was learns to question his own male role. (How can I be a good father if I'm a product of a defective male?) Male/female bashing isn't something an effective parent does.

THE BRADY BUNCH

Blending the Past with the Present

The most well-known blended family commentary is undoubtedly *The Brady Bunch*, so named for a husband and wife who each bring three children of their own into their remarriage. In a remarriage, each side of the new family unit brings with him/her certain facets from the past that affect the present. For example:

 STEPDAD

"My mom had the benefit of a single older brother who became extremely involved in our lives at the time of my parents' divorce. My sister, brother, and I considered Uncle Don to be our 'stepdad' in a way. He was always there for us."
—Ryan, Kearny, New Jersey

- Between remarried spouses there are friends, business contacts, possessions, etc., that were acquired independently of the other spouse. How will you deal with these relationships? Furniture, paintings, and other home decorations you did not pick out are also fodder for discussion.
- Between blended siblings, habits, possessions, and routines can be sources of major frustration. The simple idea of Peter leaving the toilet seat up in a family setting previously dominated by Marsha, Cindy, Jan, and Mom can be a major issue, especially for teens.

The key is to patiently and openly communicate with one another when the past comes to haunt the present. Communication can often stop a potential problem before it starts.

THE SOUND OF MUSIC

Family Roles

Even the silver screen took on the challenge of unraveling the traditional family. Widowed Captain VonTrapp hires Maria (played by Julie Andrews) from the local nunnery as a nanny for his children and eventually they fall in love and marry.

Part of the humor in the movie is Maria's discovery of what a family therapist might deem the family roles and patterns. In much the same way, a spouse entering a blended family might initially. . .

- feel intimidated or confused by inside family jokes, normal routines, and other preconceived patterns.
- perceive the situation as passing "privileged information" and act offended.

The best response is to be patient during this time of role adjustment—in time you'll develop your own lingo.

Maria also initially shares her love of music with the children. It turns out to be a bittersweet moment, as music was the hallmark of his former wife. What blended family hasn't encountered the same tensions of new ver-sus old family roles? What's a family to do?

Don't expect your spouse to pretend he or she wasn't married before. Pictures, old mutual acquaintances, family reunions, etc., are potential sore spots. Your attitude is crucial to your new family's successful maneuvering.

Do provide children the freedom to enjoy a positive relationship with or memory of their biological parent.

THE PARENT TRAP

When Children Refuse to Let Go of What Used to Be

Don't miss the realistic point of this movie in light of its unrealistic plot! It exposes the tenacity with which some children hold on to the past and their refusal to accept the new family form that a blended marriage has produced.

Children often blame themselves for a divorce or even (with younger children especially) a parent's death. They believe they had the power to send the first spouse away and now want to exercise that "power" again to reverse the tragedy by rejecting the new spouse.

The Parent Trap's hilarious scenes of the twins' terrorist antics on behalf of their single father's poor female companions are likely reminiscent of any single parent's dating life at one point or another.

IT'S NOT THE KIDS' FAULT

Remember, *your* relationship with your spouse may have been severed by divorce, but it's not necessarily so with your children.

DEPRESSING

"When my dad and my mom divorced, I was convinced if I had been a better son, if I had taken out the trash the first time dad asked me to, they would still be together. If my mom or dad ever remarries it will be so sad for me, I think. It'll be depressing to think they're really not going to get back together."

—Unknown

A Kid's Guide to Ruining Your Parent's Date:

- Be folding your dad's underwear (the ones with holes in 'em) on the couch when they come in from the evening.
- Fake roof-shaking snoring in the middle of the den floor when they return for a cup of coffee and refuse to be "woken up."
- Advise your dad's date to "ignore it like we always do" if Dad happens to do his routine gas-pass at the dinner table that night.
- Casually ask your mom as they're going out the door: "Hey, whatever happened to what's-his-name...the one with the tattoos?"

CONSIDERING REMARRIAGE?

Although there is much to be considered in a remarriage, here are some target areas:

- Have I taken stock of my financial, emotional, and personal well-being and been pleased with the results? Marriage may enhance these areas but should never be used to solve problems in these areas I can't face alone.
- How will the age of my children affect their adjustment to a new family? Is the time right? Is it too soon?
- What specifically am I looking for in a potential mate? Make a list and check it twice.
- What did I learn about myself when I was single?
- What are my greatest fears when I think about getting remarried?
- What are my expectations for a potential new partner? Are they

ASK AROUND

Ask friends and family members who have remarried about their fears and struggles. Observe the way new family roles and patterns have evolved in a remarriage scenario. Learn all you can before you take the leap!

too high to be humanly possible? A divorced person who remarries naturally expects a better product than the first go-around. This "trading up" mentality is sneaky—be sure to be realistic.

INCORPORATING THE EXTENDED FAMILY

When you marry a person, you marry into a whole new extended family unit. Here are some things to consider:

- If the former spouse has partial custody of your new spouse's kids, you will share the parenting role with them and/or their family.
- If you and your spouse both have children from other marriages, you will share in the often painstaking, not necessarily painful, process of who celebrates at whose house this year for holidays and birthdays.
- If you have a wedding or a graduation, you will share in the potential burden and blessing of having another whole set of grandparents, aunts, and uncles whom your spouse brings in from a former marriage.

MORE THAN A PIECE OF PAPER

The role of a parent can be filled automatically with a marriage license. However, the right to parent takes time to fill. Be patient as you earn the right to influence.

Don't expect your new spouse to jump right in and be the "heavy" with your children. In fact, setting up a spouse in a heavy-handed disciplinarian role during the period of initial adjustment can be devastating to the fragile relationship between the child and the new parent.

SCRIPTURE INDEX

NOTES

Look for all of the
BIBLE GUIDES FOR LIFE
from Barbour Publishing

These easy-to-understand, graphically-enhanced references provide information, inspiration. . .and fun!

BIBLE 101: provides an overview of all 66 Bible books, improves knowledge of Bible words and doctrines, and makes the Word of God come to life.

DATING 101: explains personal preparation, spiritual attitudes, meeting potential dates, dating etiquette, and much more.

MARRIAGE 101: explains the stages of marriage, languages of love, "battle of the sexes," how to keep love and romance alive, and much more.

MONEY 101: explains budgets, saving and investing, tithing, taxes, loans and debt, attitudes toward money, and much more.

Available wherever Christian books are sold.